# Vegetarian Student

*by the same author*

THE STUDENT'S COOKBOOK
SIMPLY FISH
SIMPLE FRENCH CUISINE

# VEGETARIAN
# STUDENT

## Jenny Baker

*faber and faber*

LONDON · BOSTON

First published in 1986 by
Faber and Faber Limited
3 Queen Square WC1N 3AU

Photoset by Parker Typesetting Service Leicester
Printed in England by Clays Ltd, St Ives plc

A CIP record for this book is available
from the British Library

ISBN 0-571-14525-6

6 8 10 9 7 5

*For James
who was never forgotten
but sometimes
grumbled*

# ❧ CONTENTS ❧

# ❧ INTRODUCTION ❧

It was while I was writing *The Student's Cookbook* that I knew I wanted to do a sequel which would be specifically for all those students who enjoy vegetarian food and would like more detailed information. This is the result. It can be used by strict vegetarians or by anyone who likes the idea of experimenting and eating vegetarian food some of the time.

It's only fair to tell you that although I love vegetarian food, I am not a vegetarian. However, the more I discover about the diet, the more impressed I become. Far from being dull and somehow puritanical as many non-vegetarians believe, it is full of delicious surprises. The concept of vegetarianism is a comparatively modern one but meat-free dishes have been the staple foods of many countries for centuries. You can choose from the pastas and pizzas of Italy; omelettes, quiches and vegetable gratins from France; hummus and falafel from the Middle East; chilli sauces and tortillas from Mexico; couscous from North Africa; robust bean soups and stews from all over the world. Beans and nuts can be fashioned into tasty burgers or used as stuffings for vegetables like green peppers, courgettes or tomatoes. You'll find ideas for these and lots of other dishes without too many hard-and-fast rules but, instead, plenty of ways to devise and invent your own recipes. Cooking is creative and although lists of ingredients are obviously helpful, it's no fun if the list becomes an absolute and there's no room for manoeuvre.

A vegetarian diet is recognized to be just as complete as any other provided you follow a few simple rules, as discussed in 'Vegetarian Know-How', (p.15). Indeed, there are many who would argue that it is a healthier diet than most with its emphasis on lots of fresh fruit and vegetables, wholemeal breads and grains, oils such as soya and sunflower, small amounts of honey or molasses in place of refined sugars, lentils and beans, and a moderate use of dairy foods and eggs.

As a student, cost is obviously uppermost in your mind. Vegetarian food is relatively cheap so this is a definite plus. Some of the things I recommend are more expensive than their alternatives: for example, peanut butter from wholefood sources is dearer than the hydrogenated commercial variety. The choice is up to you and if money is really tight, you will obviously have to go for the cheaper option, but it's certainly worth buying the better quality when times are less hard.

I won't waste any more of your precious time on the Introduction. Spare a few moments to read 'Vegetarian Know-How' and then start cooking.

*Bon appetit!*

# Part 1

# BASICS

# 🍃VEGETARIAN KNOW-HOW🍃

Let's take the mystique out of vegetarianism. It is as simple to follow as any other diet but you'll meet critics who'll beset you with gloomy warnings about not getting enough protein, and others who'll make cracks about the effects of eating beans and the absurdity of nut cutlets. Ignore all these Jeremiahs.

If you are new to this way of eating, begin with things you already know like pasta, pizzas or egg-based dishes. Gradually, try different grains, nuts and seeds and add pulses one kind at a time. This way your tastebuds and digestion will adapt happily. As with any diet, make it as varied as possible so that you can be reasonably sure you are getting all the necessary nutrients. Eat plenty of fresh vegetables and fruit; go for wholemeal breads and pastas and brown rather than white rice; and don't be afraid of trying things which may at first strike you as unusual like millet or tofu.

It's a moot point as to whether eating three meals a day is most beneficial. Opinion has become far less rigid. You don't really need to think in these straitjacket terms but you will feel more energetic and able to face the world if you have something before you start the day. Eat when you feel hungry rather than waiting until you are so famished you gorge yourself to bursting. If you fancy small snacks, base them on fruit, raw vegetables, nuts and seeds, wholemeal bread for sandwiches, or yoghurt with fresh or dried fruit.

## PROTEIN

Don't be alarmed by those warnings of insufficient protein. Vegetarian foods will provide all the proteins you need, provided you combine food from one main source with food from another. The diagram shows the three main sources.

**1**
**Pulses**
This includes all forms of
dried lentils and beans,
and peanuts

**2**
**Grains, nuts and seeds**
This includes all forms of
grain and by-products like
bread, pasta and flour

**3**
**Dairy foods or eggs**
This includes milk and all
by-products like cheese, yoghurt
and skimmed milk powder

Protein foods should be eaten every day and ideally at every meal. Here are some simple examples.

*Groups 1 and 2*
Peanut butter on bread
Lentils with rice
Beans on toast

*Groups 2 and 3*
Pasta with cheese
Muesli with milk and yoghurt
Quiche (with pastry, eggs mixed with curd cheese)

*Groups 3 and 1*
Curd cheese with bean soup
Mayonnaise and yoghurt dressing mixed with chickpea salad
Beansprouts with scrambled eggs

Most of these combinations seem to form quite naturally and you will very soon get used to planning your meals in this way. You can eat something from all three sources if you wish but if you only eat from one, the protein that it contains will not be fully assimilated. The two sources need not be part of the same dish, just part of the same meal, so you could eat, say, rice with stir-fried vegetables followed by cheese or yoghurt.

## CARBOHYDRATES

These provide energy. Sugar is pure carbohydrate without nutrients, it gives you a brief energy boost but nothing else other than making you fat and causing tooth decay.

Carbohydrates are best obtained from vegetables (especially root vegetables), nuts, fruit, pulses and grains, all of which also supply valuable vitamins, minerals and fibre. Fruit (fresh and dried) can be used instead of sugar to sweeten breakfast cereals and yoghurt, or use a little honey or molasses. Don't worry about bread and potatoes making you fat: they are now judged not guilty on that charge, and are good providers of nutrients and fibre.

Fibre is now recognized as essential. It prevents constipation, and helps keep teeth and gums healthy by making you chew. The vegetarian diet is high in fibre, so there's no need to take it in extra ways like bran.

## FATS

Fat is needed for concentrated energy and to assimilate certain vitamins (A,D,E and K). However, it is considered advisable to cut down on intake of saturated fat, and use instead fats and oils which are high in polyunsaturated fat. Saturated fats are found in meat and dairy produce. Polyunsaturated fats are present in many vegetable sources, although some, like coconut and palm oil, are high in saturated fat (these are often used in unspecified vegetable oils).

To confuse the issue further, many margarines, especially hard kinds, and vegetable oils and fats are hydrogenated. This process hardens and stabilizes them but also increases their saturated-fat content and destroys some nutrients. Watch out also for hydrogenated fats and oils in bought cakes, pastries, puddings and sauces.. You'll find that cold-pressed oils, obtainable mostly from wholefood or health shops, have not been hydrogenated; they are expensive but you may prefer them.

To gain the most benefit and the least ill from the fats you consume, read labels. Buy oils labelled 'high in polyunsaturates', such as sunflower, soya and corn. Use low-fat spreads and polyunsaturated margarines. Bake with pure vegetable fat.

If you want to decrease your intake of saturated fats still further, use butter sparingly and buy low-fat cheeses like cottage or curd or medium-fat rather than high-fat kinds. Many cheeses especially continental varieties are labelled with their fat content. Hard English cheeses are normally high, but low-fat equivalents are being produced. Try semi-skimmed or skimmed milk and use yoghurt or smetana in place of cream.

The following table is intended as a quick reference to show vegetarian sources of protein, carbohydrates and fats.

| Protein | Carbohydrates | Fats |
| --- | --- | --- |
| dairy produce | | dairy produce |
| eggs | | eggs |
| | fruit | |
| grains | grains | grains |
| nuts and seeds | nuts and seeds | nuts and seeds |
| pulses | pulses | |
| | vegetables (especially root) | vegetable fats and oils |

## VEGANS

A vegan diet takes the concept of vegetarianism a stage further. Dairy produce and eggs are excluded but sufficient protein is obtained by combining foods from Groups 1 and 2 on page 16. Soya beans contain complete protein and soya milk and curds (tofu) can be used in place of dairy equivalents. There is more information about soya beans on pages 84–5.

It is possible to suffer from a vitamin $B^{12}$ deficiency if following a strict vegan diet, or if only small amounts of dairy foods and eggs are eaten. Lack of $B^{12}$ can cause pernicious anaemia, so it is important to make sure you include it in your diet. It can be obtained from by-products of brewer's yeast (not to be confused with baking yeast which if eaten raw could destroy B vitamins) such as:

1   yeast extract, which can be used as a spread or to flavour soups and other dishes;

2   powdered yeast, although no one seems to like this very much; follow the instructions on the packet;

3   yeast tablets.

If you feel very tired or stressed, vitamin-yeast tablets will give you a quick boost. Obviously, if symptoms persist consult a doctor.

# ❧ SOME FOOD BUYS ❧

Many of the foods you need can be bought in ordinary shops and supermarkets. It is also worth searching out wholefood shops and warehouses, and health shops with a high turnover in pulses, cereals, nuts and seeds as these are more likely to be fresh. When you have time, browse around delicatessens, oriental and Asian shops, or those selling produce from Turkey, Greece or the Caribbean. You will find some interesting canned vegetables, spices and herbs and often a cheaper source of pulses and grains. If you don't know how to cook or prepare what you see, ask the owner; mostly they will love to teach you. If you have a friendly greengrocer who will sell you small quantities, this is a boon. Otherwise, patronize a supermarket where you can pick and weigh your own fruit and vegetables. That way you can buy exactly what you want and can forget pounds or kilos. Markets are good hunting grounds but beware of the stallholder whose display is eye-catching but who digs out less attractive goods from the back.

If possible, store pulses and grains in airtight containers. Glass storage jars are ideal and might be found at jumble sales or charity shops. If you use a fridge, keep everything covered to prevent the smell of one food affecting the taste of another and also to prevent things drying out. Store fruit and vegetables in a cool, dark place or in the lower part of a fridge. Potatoes go green and become toxic if kept in the light and bananas turn black if stored in a fridge.

Below are notes on some of the things you will be buying.

*Bread*  Go for wholemeal rather than white breads. Wholemeal and wholewheat breads contain the whole grain which includes the wheatgerm, bran, vitamins, oils and inner white starch. White bread contains the inner white starch but nearly all the wheatgerm and bran are discarded in the milling.

Certain, but not all, vitamins and minerals are artificially put back, but with the loss of the germ and bran, most of the fibre has been removed. Wheatmeal bread is made from 85 per cent extraction flour which means it has less wheatgerm, bran (fibre) and other nutrients than wholemeal. Some bread has extra bran and wheatgerm added to the flour and this is sold as granary bread. Or you may come across high-bran or wheatgerm bread, which as their names imply have added bran or wheatgerm. As a change, look out for rye breads which are much darker and closer textured than wheat bread. Or try continental breads with seeds such as caraway, poppy or sesame.

Some small bakers make good bread but supermarkets can also be a reliable source. Read wrappers and labels – some brown breads contain only a minute portion of wholemeal flour.

*Carob* This is a useful substitute for chocolate as it contains no caffeine and is slightly sweet. It can be bought in powder or block form. There are two sorts, light and dark. Dark carob has been roasted and is quite bitter, so try and buy light carob. You can use light carob in the same proportions as cocoa or chocolate. Use half as much of the dark.

*Cheese* Many cheeses are made with animal rennet, so if this worries you, read labels to make sure vegetable rennet has been used.

Curd cheese is sometimes sold as quark, a white, soft, low-fat cheese either packed in cartons or wrapped in clear plastic. Mozzarella and ricotta are curd cheeses and you can make your own curd cheese from yoghurt (see p.138). Cottage cheese is also soft and white but it has a lumpy texture.

Store cheese covered in the fridge. The flavour improves if you take it out half an hour before you need it. Use it within 4–5 days.

*Eggs* If you're unhappy about battery farming, buy free-range eggs. They are more expensive but are produced more humanely. Store eggs for up to two weeks in the kitchen, longer in the fridge.

*Fats*   Look for polyunsaturated margarines like sunflower or soya. Those sold in wholefood or health shops contain fewer additives but are more expensive than commercial brands. You can use margarine instead of butter in most recipes, although butter is sometimes preferred for its special flavour. The choice is yours. (Unsalted butter is especially creamy and delicious.) Keep them in a cool place. See page 17 for more notes on fats.

*Flour*   Stoneground wholemeal flour contains all the wheat-germ, bran and natural nutrients of the grain so it is to be preferred to white flour from which all the germ, bran and much of the nutrients have been milled (some of the nutrients but not all will have been artificially replaced by the miller). If you find the texture of wholemeal flour too heavy, you can use it half and half with white flour, or use 85 per cent extraction flour which is lighter but less nutritious having had some of the bran, wheatgerm and nutrients removed. I find wholemeal self-raising flour gives good results in most recipes. Otherwise add 1 teaspoon baking powder to every mug of plain flour. Pancakes are tasty made with buckwheat flour, although they will be heavier.

*Dried fruit*   This contains a lot of natural sugar and is much to be preferred to canned fruits which are usually in heavy syrup (although some manufacturers are producing canned fruit in unsweetened juice). Buy dried fruit in small quantities and store in a dark, cool place.

*Garlic*   If you like garlic, use it. If it appals you, leave it out. If you don't want your breath to smell, try getting just a subtle taste by rubbing a cut clove around the cooking pot or salad bowl. Garlic is credited with various wonderful qualities like the ability to cure colds, act as an antiseptic, clear pimples and aid digestion. But if you like it, you'll eat it anyway without caring about these extra incentives. You buy heads of garlic in which each segment is called a clove. It can be finely chopped, or crushed, or used whole. If you can't get the heads, you might find garlic flakes, which are strong, or powder which is very mild.

*Grains* Store any grains in a cool, dry place in airtight containers. They will keep for about 2 months. You'll find some in ordinary shops, but the widest selection will be in wholefood or health shops.

*Herbs* These elevate cooking from the bland to the sublime but should be used with discretion. Dried herbs especially have pungent flavours. The herbs most often called for are bay leaves, sweet basil, marjoram, mint, oregano (a wild form of marjoram but less sweet and stronger flavoured), parsley, rosemary, sage, and thyme. Fresh herbs are best but dried are easily found and will keep for 3–6 months; buy them first in small screw-top jars and then replenish supplies with the cheaper packets. Fresh coriander appears in some recipes; its flavour is strong and quite bitter, so use it sparingly until you acquire the taste. You can buy it in Asian shops or delicatessens as well as from some greengrocers.

*Milk* Best kept in the fridge or other cool place. Light kills the vitamins, so an outside window-sill is not ideal.

Skimmed-milk powder is a useful standby: you reconstitute it by adding water. Use it in cooking and yoghurt making.

*Miso* This is made from fermented soya beans and is used as a flavouring. It is very salty so one block lasts for ages and it keeps indefinitely. There are three kinds: *hacho*; *mugi* made from a mix of soya and barley; and *kome* made from soya and rice.

*Nuts* May seem expensive but go a long way. Store in airtight containers. Broken nuts are good value. Wholefood, health and Asian shops are good suppliers, as well as supermarkets and other grocers and greengrocers.

*Oils* Sunflower and corn are pleasant for cooking or in salads; soya oil has a stronger flavour. Other oils like olive or sesame are expensive but delicious. Look out for those oils labelled high in polyunsaturates. (See p.17.)

*Pasta* This is available made from wholemeal or white flour; you'll find the best selection of shapes in wholefood and health shops. Look out for pasta made from buckwheat, more expensive but rich in B vitamins. Dried pasta keeps indefinitely; eat fresh pasta the day you buy it.

*Peanut butter*  Sold in wholefood and health shops made with natural oil. The cheaper, commercial varieties are made from hydrogenated oils which prevent separation but reduce nutrients and increase saturated-fat levels. If peanut butter separates, a quick stir will remedy it.

*Pulses*  These are cheaper if bought in bulk and shared out with friends. Store them in airtight containers. They have a long shelf life but the older they are, the longer they will take to cook. Wholefood, health and Asian shops sell a great variety. Any sold loose need plenty of washing and picking over for stones and grit.

*Salt*  Use sparingly. Manufactured foods contain a lot of salt so cut down on what you add to food and cooking. It is doubtful that any kind of salt is better than another.

*Soy sauce*  Used as a flavouring. Look out for those made from fermented whole beans, not the sort made from extract of beans which also contain added colourings like caramel. Best buys include shoyu, tamari, or superior soy. They are sold in wholefood and health shops as well as oriental shops. The more widely available brands sold in supermarkets and other shops are of inferior quality, but, of course, cheaper.

*Seeds*  These are often used to add spice to dishes but some, like sesame, sunflower and pumpkin, are lovely sprinkled over salads, in muesli or as part of toppings to gratins. Don't be alarmed at the price, you only use a little at a time and they are a great way to add extra goodness. Alfalfa seeds are delicious sprouted.

*Spices*  Used like herbs to flavour and add interest to your cooking. Buy them whole or powdered. You can grind whole spices yourself if you have a mortar and pestle, and some recipes call for them to be used whole. The powdered kind have a shorter shelf life. Buy them in small screw-topped jars and replenish with those sold in packets.

Asian shops are usually the cheapest source. The following

spices are all included in the book, but buy them as you need them:

Aniseed and Caraway are used to flavour pulse dishes and to flavour teas.

Cinnamon is useful powdered for baking but is also sold in twills or, more cheaply, as pieces of the bark from which it is made; the latter is available from Asian shops.

Coriander is slightly sweet.

Cumin seeds give curry dishes one of their most distinctive flavours.

Dill and fennel seeds can both be used to flavour pulse dishes or flavour teas.

Ginger is used powdered for baking but fresh ginger root is much nicer for stir frying and other dishes (if you can't find it in supermarkets or at your greengrocer's, try Chinese or other Asian shops); cut off what you need – the root heals itself and keeps a long time.

Nutmeg is used powdered for baking, but whole nutmeg which you grate gives a richer flavour. (Mace, which is more expensive, is the outer husk of the nutmeg.)

Pepper is available in many different forms: black or white peppercorns to be ground in a peppermill are subtler and nicer than powdered pepper; cayenne or red pepper is very fiery; chilli powder is a mixture of different peppers and is less fiery than cayenne; paprika is made from sweet peppers (as opposed to the hot chilli peppers used for cayenne) and is mild and often used to add colour as well as flavour.

Turmeric colours everything a golden yellow and is sold in powdered form.

*Sweeteners* Best used very sparingly. All sugar, including brown, is full of carbohydrates (see page 17). Molasses is the residue from refined sugar, contains some minerals and vitamins and has a pronounced flavour. Try and find pure flower honey, not that made by bees fed on sugar; the most reliable sources for this will be wholefood and health shops, or a beekeeper you know. Use thick honey as a spread, runny for cooking.

*Tomatoes, Italian canned* Full of flavour and invaluable when fresh tomatoes are expensive. Italian tomato purée is also handy.

*Vegetables*   These are best bought in small quantities and eaten as fresh as possible. Dried vegetables such as peppers, onions, peas and mushrooms are useful store standbys. Frozen vegetables are preferable to canned which may contain additives. If you check labels you will find that many imported canned goods are additive-free. Store fresh vegetables in a cool, dark place.

*Vinegar*   This will be most useful for salad dressings. Cider-apple vinegar made from whole apples is good but expensive; otherwise go for cider or wine vinegars (malt is strong and only suitable for pickling).

*Yeast*   Can be used as a spread in the form of yeast extract or to add flavour to soups and other dishes. It is salty, so use it sparingly; varieties sold in wholefood and health shops are low on additives. Yeast used for baking is sold powdered or in block form (live yeast) and can be bought in wholefood and health shops as well as from private bakers. Dried fast-action yeast saves time.

*Yoghurt*   Many commercial brands are thickened with animal rennet, most contain additives, colouring and are over-sweetened, so buy natural yoghurts and read the labels carefully. It's easy to make your own – a recipe is on page 138. Try the Greek yoghurts made from goat's or ewe's milk, they are thick and creamy and make lovely cheese (see page 140).

# 🍂 SOME EQUIPMENT 🍂

If you are new to cooking, you'll be all at sea when it comes to buying equipment. There is so much choice, and new gadgets are constantly being added to the range in the shops. You will soon discover that you tend to rely on a few tried and trusted ones and that a huge assortment is unnecessary.

First is a list of what I think are basic essentials, followed by a list of things to buy gradually as and when you need them, and finally, some suggestions for adding to a Christmas or birthday present list or perhaps persuading someone to buy you as a going-away-from-home present.

## BASIC ESSENTIALS

As all the recipes in this book are based on mug and spoon measurements, you will need:

*Half-pint mug*   Most mass-produced mugs hold half a pint or you could use a beer mug.

*Measuring spoons*   A standard set including a tablespoon (15 ml) and teaspoon (5 ml).

*Can opener*

*Chopping board*   Go for melamine or a really stout wooden board. If you want to use it for rolling out pastry it should be quite big.

*Egg slice*   Non-stick, if you are using non-stick pans. It has a thousand uses including turning omelettes, pancakes, eggs, fried sandwiches, etc.

*Frying pan*   An 18 cm (7-inch) frying pan would serve most of your needs and one with a non-stick coating would be useful. Metal implements must not be used with this type or they will damage the surface. Choose a pan with a heavy base. If you are likely to be cooking for more than one, you might need a larger pan, say 25 cm (10 inch), although a wok could substitute. See below.

*Grater*   The box-shaped kind is most useful as it will grate and slice. A *Mouli cheese-grater* can also be used for chopping small amounts of nuts.

*Knives*   At least one very sharp cook's knife. It's worth buying the best you can afford. Stainless steel knives, although somewhat frowned upon by the purists, do have the advantage of being cheaper than carbon steel knives and will not leave a black stain when cutting fruit or vegetables; also, they do not rust. They blunt more easily, however, so it is necessary to have a *knife sharpener*, either a steel or the kind with two short, ribbed crossed rods.

*Saucepans*   Two is the minimum, a small one of about 1-litre (2-pint) capacity and a large one of about 3-litre (6-pint) which will be used for soups, cooking pasta, etc. A third in between these two sizes would also be useful. Buy pans with heavy bases, either non-stick or enamel. Cheap, thin pans burn easily and are a bore to wash up.

*Shallow heatproof dish*   This is needed for such dishes as stuffed vegetables, gratins, etc. Choose one that can go in the oven or under a grill. Can be glass, earthenware or metal, about 1-litre (2-pint) size.

*Strainer*   You could settle for a colander, or a mesh sieve with a handle which can also be used for sifting flour. Or you could make do with a slotted spoon.

*Vegetable peeler*   Look out for the swivel-bladed variety. This is an extremely handy gadget which, once you have mastered the technique of peeling away from yourself with quick, light strokes, can be used not only for peeling, but also for slicing cheese and cutting vegetables into thin strips for salads.

*Wok*   This Chinese cooking vessel with its rounded base and wide shape is extremely useful not only for stir-frying but also for braising and cooking all sorts of sauces. If you buy one from a Chinese shop it will probably be much cheaper. It comes with a lid and separate base which helps to keep it stable on the stove.

*Wooden spoon, fork and spatula*   Very cheap, very useful.

## EXTREMELY USEFUL

*Baking sheet*   You need this for pizzas, baking potatoes, putting under quiche tins to make the pastry crisp, baking loaves, etc.

*Bowl*   For mixing, beating, etc. You might already have decided on a bowl for your mortar, see below. As well as a half-litre (1-pint) size, you might find a larger mixing bowl handy.

*China cocotte dishes*   You can find these small dishes in kitchen shops, they are good for steaming or baking eggs.

*China teapot*   (Makes nicer tea than a metal pot.) You might be able to find a china tea-infuser for herb teas; this consists of a mug with its own built-in strainer and a lid, called a *tisanière* in France.

*Corkscrew and bottle opener*   A universal type of corkscrew and bottle opener.

*Grill pan and grid*   Hopefully, this will be part of the stove but if not, you'll find one handy.

*Jar for sprouting pulses*   A wide-mouthed storage jar is ideal, 1-litre (2-pint) size. You can also use it for suspending cheese while it is draining (see yoghurt cheese page 140). Jars are often found at jumble sales.

*Loaf tin*   1-litre (2-pint) size for gratins, savoury loaves, bread, etc.

*Measuring jug*   These are sold with solid as well as liquid measures. Not strictly necessary for this book but will save you time if you're working from other recipes.

*Mortar and pestle*   For mashing, puréeing, grinding spices, crushing garlic. A small one is useful but if you can find a mortar which holds half a litre (1 pint), you can use it for making spreads, beating eggs and small mixing jobs. (I find an earthenware mortar with a wooden pestle is ideal.) If you can find a strong pestle you could use it with an ordinary pudding-shaped basin in either china or strong glass.

*Mouli-légumes* This gadget looks a little like one of those old-fashioned mincers. It sits over a bowl or saucepan, and has three separate grating discs. It can be used for a variety of tasks including making breadcrumbs, puréeing, sieving flour.

*Muslin or cheesecloth* For sprouting beans (see page 95) or draining cheese (see page 140). You can buy half a metre or less at material counters. You could always use a J-cloth.

*Nylon scouring pad or brush* Useful for scrubbing vegetables.

*Pasta server* This is a specially shaped spoon with spikes which makes serving pasta easy. They are sold in wood or plastic.

*Peppermill* Once you've tasted freshly milled black or white pepper, you won't be able to go back to the powdered variety.

*Potato baker* Potatoes are impaled on spikes and cooking time reduced by about 15 minutes. A stainless steel fork can be used for the same purpose.

*Rolling pin* Or you could use a bottle.

*Rubber spatula* For scraping the last morsel out of a pot. The rubber variety is superior to those made in plastic or wood because of its flexibility.

*Scissors* Useful for opening milk and other cartons, as well as chopping herbs.

*Timer* Allows you to get on with something else and forget what's cooking.

*Tin or ring* For baking, an 18-cm (7-inch) removable-base tin, or a ring which you use on a baking sheet.

*Whisk* A balloon-shaped wire whisk is useful for making

sauces, beating batters, making mayonnaise, etc. A fork will do but takes more effort.

*Wide-mouthed vacuum flask* For making yoghurt or taking soup with you for lunch. You'll probably find the ½-litre (1-pint) size most useful.

## PRESENT LIST

*Food processor* This could prove a boon, although you should bear in mind the space it will take up and it can be a bore to clean if you only use it to chop a tablespoon of nuts. However, as its uses include chopping, grating, mixing, blending, making pastry and bread, mincing and puréeing you could well find you use it every day, especially if there are several people sharing meals.

*Liquidizer or blender* Cheaper than a food processor but if it is to chop nuts, it must be a strong one. It is useful for all blending, puréeing and chopping jobs.

*Grinder* A small, strong electric coffee grinder would be useful for chopping nuts and seeds, grinding spices, etc.

*Kettle* A jug-type electric kettle saves on fuel and stove space so might be a useful gadget to keep in your room.

*Multicooker* Especially designed for people with limited cooking facilities. You can use it for frying, grilling, baking, making sauces, cooking vegetables, etc.

# ❦ QUANTITIES AND TEMPERATURES ❦

Nearly all the recipes are aimed at one person cooking for themselves but some are definitely for more and this is stated. You can always increase quantities but be careful how much extra seasoning you add, you won't need twice as much when preparing, say, for two; it's best to taste as you go. Obviously some people eat more than others, so you may need to adjust amounts to suit your appetite.

## MEASURING QUANTITIES

Scales are not necessarily going to be part of your equipment so I have measured the quantities needed in most recipes using a mug and different-sized spoons. It isn't essential to use exact quantities, although *proportions* should be correct when baking or judging how much water in which to cook grains. You'll find the mug and spoon sizes given in the list of basic equipment. Sometimes it is definitely more helpful to have actual solid weights or liquid measures and where I think this is so, I have given both their metric and imperial equivalents. It isn't practical to give exact conversions as for example 1 ounce equals 28.3 g so an approximate figure is given. If you ever follow recipes that list ingredients in both imperial and metric measures, follow one set only.

*Level spoons and mugs*  The measures are based on level spoons and mugs and when it is essential to make sure you have an exact measure, for example, when making pastry, fill the mug or spoon and level the top by taking the blade of a knife across it.

*A pinch*  Is just that, the amount you can hold between the top of your finger and thumb.

## OVEN TEMPERATURES

Oven temperatures are given for gas regulo marks, electric Fahrenheit and Celsius.

| | Gas | °Fahrenheit | °Celsius |
|---|---|---|---|
| Very low | 1/4 | 225 | 110 |
| | 1/2 | 250 | 120 |
| Low | 1 | 275 | 140 |
| | 2 | 300 | 150 |
| Moderate | 3 | 325 | 160 |
| | 4 | 350 | 180 |
| Moderately hot | 5 | 375 | 190 |
| | 6 | 400 | 200 |
| Hot | 7 | 425 | 220 |
| | 8 | 450 | 230 |
| Very hot | 9 | 475 | 240 |

## SOME NOTES ON ECONOMY

It is cheaper to use a burner on the stove rather than the grill, and grilling is cheaper than using the oven. It is therefore always worth trying to cook more than one thing when using the oven.

Heat is retained by electric ovens and burners so they go on cooking for a few minutes when you turn them off.

Electric ovens need pre-heating for about 10 minutes. It's up to you whether you pre-heat a gas oven, but if not add about 10 minutes to the cooking time.

You'll save time and fuel if you cover saucepans which you are bringing to the boil.

# Part 2

# ACTION

# ANYTIME BREAKFAST

Breakfast is the meal you snatch between matching a pair of socks, grabbing a comb to your hair and dashing out of the door in the morning, but it is also a meal to eat at any time of the day when you don't feel like cooking and are distinctly peckish.

The easiest thing is to cut a slice of bread and spread it with something, so lay in a small stock of interesting toppings. Peanut butter or yeast extract are obvious choices, but try covering the peanut butter with honey, a mashed banana or a few raisins or sultanas. Top yeast extract with curd or cottage cheese, sprinkled, if you like, with a few sesame seeds. Try Swiss yeast extract pâté sold in health shops; it's pricey but one tube goes a long way. Add a few slices of cucumber or tomato, or top the lot with a small handful of beansprouts, quite cheap bought in packets but even cheaper if you grow your own, (see page 95).

If you like jam or marmalade, look out for those which are less sweetened and not too full of colouring or preservatives. A kind aunt or other relative who makes jam or marmalade will probably be only too pleased to give you a jar or two, or you could go to a few charity fairs or church bazaars – good hunting grounds for home-made preserves. Try the continental fruit spreads made from pressed fruits like apple and pear; you'll find them in wholefood and health shops. Buy hummus (made from chickpeas and sesame seeds) or use some of your own bean spreads (see recipes on page 44).

FRUIT

Now's the time to eat some fresh fruit. Apples and bananas are good standbys and available throughout the year but why not make life more interesting by buying other fruits in season when they are plentiful and cheap? In winter buy juicy pears, or tangerines such as seedless satsumas or clementines; look out for pink grapefruit, ugli fruit and blood oranges, or if you don't like pips buy navel oranges; try lychees which when freed from the outer red-tinted husk are white and tender with a musky flavour. In summer the choice is between all those exotic imported fruits or our own home-grown varieties. If you ever see white peaches, buy them; their skin is just as rosy as the more common yellow variety, but their flavour is something special. Try persimmons and mangoes; buy all kinds of grapes from the small green seedless to those which are a dusky blue-black. Try the red-fleshed water melon, yellow honeydew, green Ogen, or, for a treat, the small, lush Charentais. Eat strawberries and raspberries with curd cheese or yoghurt instead of expensive cream. Don't overlook avocado pears: half of one provides a satisfying breakfast. You can eat it sprinkled with a little lemon juice, or look for other ideas on page 117.

DRIED FRUIT SALAD

In winter when fresh fruit is scarce, it's worth having a bowl of dried fruit salad on hand. Look on the shelves of a whole-food or health shop and you'll find a huge range of dried fruits including apricots, peaches, apples, pears, bananas, figs, prunes and dates as well as sultanas, raisins and currants, or you can buy packets of mixed fruit. (See page 146 for more information.) Preparation is simplicity itself and takes only a few minutes.

Put the fruit into a bowl, cover with cold water and leave overnight. Lots of recipes suggest using boiling water, or cooking the fruit but this isn't really necessary. Keep the salad, covered, in the fridge. Eat it as it is or add a spoonful or two to cereal; drink the liquid or add it to muesli. An old trick is to add two or three teaspoons of strong China tea which gives a delicious smoky flavour. If you have no China tea, try adding herb teas such as camomile, linden or rosehip.

YOGHURT

This can make the basis of your breakfast, flavoured perhaps with chopped fruit. Once again go for seasonal fruits; there's

nothing extravagant about adding strawberries and raspberries in midsummer when apples and bananas can be quite
expensive. Yoghurt is lovely with a sprinkling of sesame
seeds or chopped nuts, mixed with dried fruit or honey, or
with a tablespoon of wheatflakes or other cereal.

FRUIT JUICE

The best fruit juice is obtained from freshly squeezed fruit.
Alas, this can be expensive and time consuming, so look out
for commercial juices without preservatives or artificial
colourings. Try mixing orange juice (or milk) with a beaten
egg, sweetened if you wish with a little honey. It may sound
strange but this is just about the easiest meal for you to grab
before you go out.

CURD OR COTTAGE CHEESE

An Italian dish is to mix ricotta cheese with a tablespoon of
made coffee, sprinkled with sugar. If you can't find ricotta,
use any curd or cottage cheese. This is also nice mixed with
fresh or dried fruit, or some chopped nuts or sesame seeds.


## MUESLI

At the turn of the century Dr Bircher Benner, who lived in
Zurich, conceived the idea of creating a meal which would
provide his patients with all the nourishment they needed in a
simple and easily digested form. He took cereal, added milk
and yoghurt, a little fruit juice and mixed it with grated apple
and chopped nuts adding a little honey as a sweetener. He
called the result Birchermuesli. It was a meal for any time of
the day, although originally it was most often eaten in the
evening. Nowadays it can be found in all sorts of different
guises on Swiss menus.

I asked my friend Margaret, a Swiss, to tell me how it was
originally made. She said that the word muesli is used to
describe all sorts of purées. It originates from the word 'muus'
which is used for baby foods – we would probably say 'mush'.
She gave me two recipes and you will see that the Swiss
version of muesli is very much sloppier than the kind to

which we are accustomed. The first recipe is based on the original, the second is the one she makes herself.

She leaves out the cereal in her own version as she finds it too heavy. (She thus breaks the rule of complementing protein, but as she has just celebrated her eighty-fifth birthday, we won't quarrel with her! It just goes to show that muesli is something with which to experiment.)

BIRCHERMUESLI

Mix 2 tablespoons oats, 2 tablespoons of milk, 1 grated apple including the core, 2 tablespoons of grated nuts, 1 tablespoon of sugar or honey, 2 tablespoons of lemon or orange juice. If too thick, add more milk or fruit juice.

MARGARET'S MUESLI

Mix half a carton of curd or cottage cheese with half a carton of yoghurt (plain or with fruit), 1 grated apple with core, 1 grated pear, 1 grated banana, a squeeze of orange and lemon juice and sugar or honey to taste.

You can buy ready-mixed muesli in all sorts of shops as well as wholefood and health shops (avoid those with added sugar), or you can buy different grains and use wheat, rye, barley or soya flakes combined with oatflakes or oatmeal. If you mix your own, make sure you add some dried fruit and nuts.

You can eat muesli as it is or if you find it too dry and chewy, try soaking it overnight in a little milk or fruit juice. Below is my basic version of muesli given as a guide to the proportions of cereal to fruit and nuts. Vary the cereals as you wish.

BASIC MUESLI

Mix 4 mugs of oatmeal with 4 mugs of wheatflakes (or other flakes), 1 mug of wheatgerm (optional but gives added nutrients), 1 mug of chopped dried fruit and 1 mug of chopped nuts. Store muesli in an airtight container.

In the morning, add milk, perhaps a little fruit juice (lemon, orange or apple) and some chopped fresh fruit. Finish with a generous dollop of yoghurt or curd cheese. Be adventurous

with your fruit: apple and banana are nice but so are strawberries, raspberries and other summer fruits, In winter, add a
spoonful of your own dried fruit salad (see page 38).

The fruit adds sweetness, so you may find you need no sugar
or honey. Choose your nuts from the huge range available in
wholefood or health shops and, if you like, toss in a handful of
seeds like sesame or sunflower.

You can even try stirring in a tablespoon of peanut butter or
tahini.

Having established a basic theme, vary it as you wish. The
only rule to follow is to base it on a mixture of cereal, milk
which can be cow, goat or soya, skimmed or not, and fresh fruit
and nuts.

CRUNCHY OR GRANOLA

If you have a passion for those packets of crunchy cereals
mixed with fruits and nuts, it is not difficult to make your own
and it might save you a bit. All you do is to mix cereal with dried
fruit and nuts – you could use the basic muesli mix. Add 1
tablespoon of oil and 1 tablespoon of honey to 1 mug of the mix.
Heat the oven to Gas 4/350°F/180°C. Spread the mixture on a
baking sheet or in a heatproof dish and put in the oven for 15
minutes. Give it a stir and return to the oven for a further 15
minutes. As soon as you take it out transfer the mix to a bowl or
it will stick. When it is cold, store it in an airtight container.

PORRIDGE

If you really fancy something warming, porridge is the
simplest answer.

½ mug of milk, or a mixture of milk and water
3 tablespoons porridge oats

Put the milk into a pan, sprinkle on the oats and bring to the
boil, stirring constantly. As soon as the mixture thickens, lower
the heat and stir for 1 minute. You can eat it at once or let it
stand for a few minutes to develop the flavour.

Sweeten porridge with either honey, molasses, dried fruit,
jam or marmalade instead of sugar. Try sprinkling a few
chopped nuts on top.

If you immediately put cold water into the pan, it won't be too bad to clean. You might be lucky and find an old-fashioned double saucepan at a jumble sale which means the porridge cooks without fear of burning in the top pan over the lower one which is partially filled with boiling water.

*Muesli porridge*  Follow the above recipe using 4 tablespoons of muesli in place of the oats.

*Carob porridge*  Sprinkle a tablespoon of carob powder on to the cooked porridge and mix it well so that it doesn't form lumps.

If you absolutely insist on an old-fashioned cooked breakfast you will find lots of ideas in the chapter 'Bread Base' under headings such as things on toast, toasted or fried sandwiches, and in the chapter 'Eggs'.

# ❧ BREAD BASE ❧

Take a slice or two of bread, eat it with eggs, dairy foods or pulses and you have the simplest possible meal which has all those desirable protein components. Add some salad or some fresh fruit and discard all feelings of guilt that you haven't gone to any trouble. Your meal will be a good one.

## SANDWICHES

The perfect lunch or easy supper! There's no need to limit yourself to conventionally sliced bread – there are all sorts of other outers such as baps, rolls and muffins, French bread sliced lengthwise, pitta bread, many of which can be found made with wholemeal flour. Search out small bakers and look in wholefood and health shops for breads made from rye, oatmeal, cornmeal and granary flours, and try breads with added seeds and nuts. Everybody has their own favourite fillings but below are a few ideas to help you.

### Sandwich fillings

*Peanut butter*   The peanut is not a nut at all but a pulse, so makes a perfect filling for sandwiches. It's worth buying peanut butter from a reliable maker (see page 24). You can use it on its own or dress it up with one of the following: honey; a few drops of soy sauce; a thin layer of miso; a squeeze of lemon juice; chopped garlic or onion; a pinch of cumin; sliced banana and honey; chopped dried fruit; a thin layer of yeast extract; chopped or sliced hardboiled egg; any sort of salad ingredient that takes your fancy (see page 45).

*Tahini*   Tahini is made from sesame seeds and is used as an ingredient in Hummus (see page 44). You can also use it as a sandwich spread on its own or with one of the following: a thin layer of miso; a tablespoon of any cooked or canned pulses; a few drops of soy sauce; chopped or sliced hardboiled egg; sliced or curd or cottage cheese; a thin layer of yeast extract. Add any sort of salad ingredient (see page 45) or some fruit such as chopped apple or sliced banana.

*Cheese*  Use any sort of cheese sliced or grated, or mix soft cheeses with different flavourings. Try goat cheeses which are pungent but delicious; you can make your own curd cheeses using yoghurt (see page 138).

As well as being a pleasant contrast to the crispness of salad ingredients (see page 45), cheese also goes well with any of the following: chopped nuts or dried fruit; pickles, especially if you are lucky enough to have been given some home-made; sliced gherkins; peanut butter or tahini; honey and sliced banana; stoned and chopped olives; capers; chopped garlic and a sprinkling of herbs; a teaspoon of soy sauce or miso.

*Hummus and pulse spreads*  Almost any cooked dried beans such as aduki, chickpeas, red kidney, lentils or haricot can be used to make a spread. It's a perfect way of using up leftovers or you can use the canned variety. Hummus, which is made with chickpeas and originates from the Middle East, is the one that is best known and can be bought from delicatessens, wholefood and health shops as well as supermarkets. It is easy to make and cheaper if you do so. Mash 4 tablespoons of cooked or canned chickpeas; you can use a mortar and pestle, or a bowl and potato masher or base of a bottle – it's easier if you do a tablespoon at a time. When you have a mush, beat in a tablespoon of water, cooking liquid or liquid from the can and a tablespoon of lemon juice. Chop or crush a clove of garlic finely and add. Stir in 2 tablespoons of tahini and a pinch of salt and pepper. If it seems too runny, add a little more tahini which will thicken it. On the other hand if it seems too thick, beat in a little oil. Store the hummus, covered, in the fridge where it will keep several days. If it dries out, beat in more oil. You may find it separates on storing, but all you need do is beat it a little.

Use any other pulse you have on hand to make a spread basing it on the method for hummus, omitting the tahini if you like. Experiment with different seasonings such as a pinch of paprika or cayenne pepper; a few chopped herbs such as mint, parsley, thyme or oregano; a few drops of soy sauce or ¼ teaspoon of miso; a teaspoon of tomato purée; chopped onion or snipped chives. You could mix in a little peanut butter, yoghurt or mayonnaise.

*Salad*   Salad ingredients add crispness and flavour to sandwiches and you can add them to almost any filling. As well as lettuce, cucumber or tomato try one of the following ideas: beansprouts; raw sliced mushrooms with perhaps a squeeze of lemon juice; finely sliced raw courgette with a teaspoon of tomato purée or soy sauce; strips of green or red pepper; grated carrot; chopped orange or satsuma with a little mint; Chinese leaves or shredded white or red cabbage; chopped apple.

PITTA BREAD

Pitta bread makes a great container for food. You can buy white or wholemeal versions. Split down the middle, the hidden pocket can hold almost any kind of sandwich filling or be used as a container for a hot sauce such as those in the pasta, pulse or vegetable sections. You can fill the pitta with a salad or scrambled eggs; and if you have a party you can serve them to your guests to fill their own thus doing away with the need for knives and forks.

TOASTED OR FRIED SANDWICHES

These make an easy supper dish. You can use any of the fillings suggested for sandwiches on the previous pages to which you could add, say, a sliced tomato, or some sliced mushrooms, or a few beansprouts. Don't forget to eat them with a salad or follow them with a piece of fresh fruit.

*Toasted sandwich*   Toast two slices of bread on one side only. Put filling between the two toasted sides and put them back under the grill to toast the other two sides. It's up to you whether you butter or margarine them before putting in the filling.

*Fried sandwich*   Heat a frying pan, spread two slices of bread with margarine or butter. Put the first slice into the pan fat-side down, add filling and second slice of bread fat-side up. When the bottom is golden, turn the sandwich and cook the second side.

Or, heat the frying pan, add two tablespoons of oil, margarine or butter and add your already made-up sandwich. Fry on both sides until golden.

*Fried sandwich with egg and milk*  Dip made-up sandwich in egg beaten with 2 tablespoons of milk coating both sides with the mixture and fry as above.

## THINGS ON TOAST

As well as obvious things like canned baked beans, eggs, sliced cheese or tomato, you can use toast as a vehicle for many of the sauces suggested as accompaniments to pasta or grains, pulses or vegetables. You could top them with grated cheese and perhaps a sprinkling of sesame seeds or chopped nuts, finishing them off under the grill just to brown and bubble the top. Eat your dish with a few beansprouts or some other salad to add crispness and interest.

### FRENCH BEANS AND NUTS ON TOAST

Cook French or runner beans as page 126. Eat them on buttered toast with a tablespoon of chopped nuts (walnuts are nice) salt, pepper, and perhaps a squeeze of lemon juice.

### ONION AND GREEN OR RED PEPPER ON TOAST

Chop an onion and a green or red pepper – discarding the seeds – and cook them in a little hot oil until soft, 5–10 minutes.

Season with salt, pepper and a teaspoon of soy sauce, and turn out on to buttered toast.

### BEANS ON TOAST

Use any cooked or canned beans such as brown lentils, aduki, chickpeas, or red kidney. Heat a tablespoon of oil in a wok or saucepan and fry a chopped onion until it is beginning to brown. Add a chopped garlic clove, a pinch of ground cumin and a pinch of ground coriander, 4 tablespoons of any cooked beans, a pinch of salt and some pepper. Eat on buttered toast. Experiment with different seasonings adding, for example, a few drops of soy sauce or a little tomato purée; or use herbs instead of the spices; or instead of cumin and coriander, substitute chilli powder or a pinch of nutmeg or ground cinnamon.

## WELSH RAREBIT AND BUCK RAREBIT

These are made by mixing about 3 tablespoons of grated cheese with ¼ teaspoon of made mustard and enough milk to make a paste (you can use beer instead). Spread the paste on toast and put it under a hot grill to bubble and brown. This makes Welsh Rarebit.

Top it with a poached egg and you have Buck Rarebit.

## MUSHROOMS ON TOAST

You can make mushrooms on toast into a gourmet dish by cooking 5–6 sliced mushrooms in a tablespoon or two of butter or oil. Keep the heat quite high and turn them over and over until they begin to change colour and shrink. Add a pinch of salt and some pepper, a pinch of nutmeg and a clove of very finely chopped garlic with either chopped parsley or thyme. Garlic breath is supposed to be cured by chewing parsley and many French and Italian dishes include a mixture of the two. Whether it has this effect is open to question but the taste is appealing.

## FRENCH TOAST OR PAIN PERDU

One of those lovely little snacks that you really have earned at the end of a hard, or not so hard, day's slog. Dip slices of bread into beaten egg thinned with a tablespoon of milk and fry them in hot oil or butter until golden on both sides. Eat with something savoury like soy sauce or sweet with a little honey or jam. You can do the same thing with sandwiches, filling them first, dipping them in the egg mixture then frying them – the result is called Poor Knights of Windsor. The name alone makes them seem delicious!

## PIZZA

A pizza base is usually made from some sort of bread dough but a scone or potato base is just as good. Bread dough is a bit of a bore to make unless you are cooking for a few but you can use a packet of bread or pizza mix, or even a scone mix. Pizzas can be cooked in the oven or a frying pan; if you use a ready-made base the whole thing can be put under a hot grill.

### GRILLED PIZZA

Choose your base from one of the following using the wholemeal kind if possible: bread; French bread slit lengthwise; half a roll, a muffin or bap or a pitta bread.

Simply spread the pizza topping (see page 49) on the base and put under a hot grill for 3–4 minutes until the cheese melts and bubbles.

### FRYING PAN PIZZA WITH A SCONE BASE

Make a scone dough (see page 50) or use a scone mix.

Sprinkle your board or table with 1–2 tablespoons of flour and roll out the dough into a round to fit your frying pan. Heat 2 tablespoons of oil in the pan and when it is hot put in the dough. Cook it over a medium heat until the base is golden (about 5 minutes). Turn it over and add the pizza topping (see page 49). Cover the pan, lower the heat and cook the pizza for about 15 minutes when the base will be golden, the topping heated through and the cheese melted. If you like it brown on top, stick it under a hot grill for a few minutes.

### FRYING PAN PIZZA WITH A POTATO BASE

Make a potato dough (see page 51). Flatten or roll the dough as in the method for the scone base above. Heat the frying pan and add 2 tablespoons of oil. When it is hot put in the dough and lower the heat. Put on the pizza topping (see page 49). Cover the pan and let it cook for about 15 minutes. If you want the cheese to be brown, put it under a hot grill for a few minutes.

OVEN PIZZA

Use a bread, scone or potato dough (see pages 50–1) or use a pizza or wholemeal bread packet mix, using the equivalent of 1 mug (175gm or 6oz) for a pizza for one or two people. Roll the dough out on a floured board into a round about 20cm across (8 inches). Heat the oven to Gas 7/425°F/220°C while you make the topping. Grease a baking sheet with a little oil or butter and lay on it the pizza base. Sprinkle over a little oil, add the topping. Put into the oven and let it cook for about 25–30 minutes.

Pizza toppings

The topping consists of three layers:
1 A layer of tomato: use 3–4 sliced fresh tomatoes; or half a can of drained Italian tomatoes, crushed; or 3–4 tablespoons of Italian pizza sauce.
   Flavour this layer with ½ teaspoon of dried oregano, marjoram or sweet basil, a pinch of salt and some pepper.
2 A main flavouring such as garlic, 1–2 cloves finely chopped; onion, finely sliced; peppers, green or red, cut in thin strips, seeds discarded; courgette, cut in thin rings; olives, black or green; sweetcorn, two or three tablespoons of canned; potato, a few slices of cooked potato; ratatouille, (see page 131); fennel, cut a bulb in four and cook it gently for five minutes in a little oil before adding to pizza; pulses, 2–3 tablespoons of cooked or canned beans.
3 A layer of cheese which can be sliced or grated: use whatever you have available. Traditionally, Mozzarella is used, but try Cheddar, Cheshire or Lancashire; curd or goat's cheese; Edam, Bel Paese, Gruyère or Emmental.
   For added interest, you could sprinkle over a handful of wheatgerm, sesame seeds or chopped nuts.

Pizza originated in Italy, of course, but it is also served extensively in the South of France where the base is rolled out until it is as thin as possible giving a very light pizza. Sometimes a pastry base is used and you may like to try this (see page 108). Also from France comes a lovely onion-based recipe called pissaladière, similar to a pizza but without any cheese. Traditionally, it includes anchovies which add a very salty, distinctive tang, but you could use miso instead.

PISSALADIÈRE (1 or 2 servings)

> 225 g (8 oz) onions
> 1 clove garlic
> 2 tablespoons oil
> ½ teaspoon oregano or thyme
> pepper
> 1 tablespoon miso
> 2 tomatoes
> 8 black olives – optional
> pizza base

Slice the onions finely. Heat the oil and cook over a very low heat in a covered pan until they become soft without browning, 15–20 minutes. Add the chopped garlic, herbs, pepper and miso and mix well. Spread on to a pizza base; top with sliced tomatoes and the olives. Cook by any of the pizza methods given above.

SCONE BASE FOR PIZZA (1–2 servings)

> 1 mug self-raising wholemeal flour (or plain wholemeal flour with 1 teaspoon baking powder)
> pinch of salt
> 1 tablespoon oil
> 2–3 tablespoons water

Sieve the flour and salt, tipping into the bowl any bran that remains behind. This process helps to lighten the dough, but if you haven't got a sieve, leave it out. Make a hollow in the middle, add the oil and 1 tablespoon of water. Mix with a knife, adding more water gradually until you have a firm and springy dough. Put some flour on your hands, to prevent the dough sticking to them, and form it into a ball. Sprinkle about 1 tablespoon of flour on to a board or table and roll out the dough into a circle to fit your pan, or, for oven pizza, to about 20 cm across (8 inches).

POTATO BASE FOR PIZZA (1–2 servings)

> 4 tablespoons mashed potato – skin and all (see page 121)
> salt and pepper
> 1 tablespoon oil
> 3 tablespoons self-raising wholemeal flour (or plain wholemeal flour with ½ teaspoon baking powder)
> 1–2 tablespoons water or milk

Using a knife, mix the mashed potato with a pinch of salt, some pepper and the oil. Add the flour and baking powder, and sufficient water or milk to form a dough. Sprinkle about 1 tablespoon of flour on to a board and roll the dough into a circle to fit your frying pan; or if baking, roll to a diameter of about 20 cm (8 inches).

BREAD DOUGH BASE FOR PIZZA (1–2 servings)

> 1 mug wholemeal flour (either plain or self-raising)
> ½ teaspoon salt
> ½ teaspoon sugar
> ½ teaspoon fast-action yeast (or use ordinary dried yeast plus 1 vitamin C tablet of 50 mg)
> ½ tablespoon oil
> 2 tablespoons boiling water mixed with 4 tablespoons cold water

Sieve flour and salt into a bowl, adding any extra bran which remains in the sieve. Stir in the sugar and fast-action yeast. (If using ordinary dried yeast and the vitamin C tablet, dissolve them in the water at this stage. The vitamin C speeds up the action; it is already present in the fast-action yeast). Make a hollow in the centre of the flour and add the oil and liquid; mix with a knife to a firm dough. Sprinkle some flour on your work surface and some on your hands to prevent the dough sticking. Form the dough into a ball and knead it for about 10 minutes until it is springy and elastic.

To knead use the heel of your hand to flatten the ball, pushing it away from you and then gathering it again into a ball. Keep repeating this process, turning the dough to distribute the yeast evenly throughout. If you've never kneaded dough before, think of the action of a cat when it's in an ecstasy of pawing and purring.

Roll or press the dough into a circle of about 20 cm (8 inches) and set it on a baking dish. Cover it, if possible, with a piece of clingfilm which will prevent the air from hardening the surface. Set it aside in a warm place for the dough to expand for about 30 minutes.

## BREAD

You can use the pizza scone and bread base mixtures to make loaves.

### QUICK OR EMERGENCY BREAD USING SCONE BASE

Double the quantities given, and use 3 teaspoons of baking powder. Heat oven to Gas 7/425°F/220°C. Make up as on page 50. Form the mixed dough into a ball. Knead it on a floured board until it feels smooth. Form into a round loaf shape and put it on a greased baking sheet.

Bake for 35 minutes. This bread should be eaten quickly as it doesn't keep as well as yeast bread.

### QUICK WHOLEMEAL BREAD

Double the quantities given for bread dough. When the dough has been kneaded, put it into a greased loaf tin, or form it into a round loaf shape and put it on a greased baking sheet. Cover it loosely with clingfilm and leave for 30 minutes in a warm place until it has risen. Bake at Gas 6/400°F/200°C for 10 minutes, then lower the heat to Gas 4/350°F/180°C for a further 40 minutes. Remove from the oven and tap the loaf. It should sound hollow; if not, return it to the oven for a bit longer.

# ❧ PASTA ❧

Pasta is a glorified flour and water paste usually enriched with egg. It is to the Italians what potatoes are to us, and is eaten with an ingenious variety of sauces. Look in any Italian cookery book and you will find an endless number of different pastas of all shapes and sizes of which every one seems to have its own specifically designed sauce. Don't be afraid of breaking with tradition; in practice you can mostly use whatever pasta you have on hand. Some sauces require absolutely no cooking while others are extremely elaborate. Many of them are vegetarian in concept, and as cheese nearly always plays a part, a perfect protein balance is achieved. Until recently pasta was always made with refined flour but it is now easily obtainable made with wholewheat or buckwheat flours.

Cheese to serve with pasta

Grated cheese is nearly always sprinkled over pasta dishes and in Italy they use a hard cheese which has matured for at least two years; the best known is Parmesan which is very expensive. Ignore the ready-grated variety sold in small cartons – it bears no resemblance to its origins and tastes more like soap. Try using hard English cheeses like Cheddar, Cheshire, Lancashire or Double Gloucester, or imported cheeses like Emmental, Gruyère, Edam or Gouda.

TO COOK PASTA

Allow 75–100 g (3–4 oz) per person of fresh or dried pasta. Use fresh pasta the day it is bought; dried will keep indefinitely.
1  Use a large pan and allow 3 mugs of water for every 100 g (4 oz) pasta.
2  Bring the water to the boil, add a pinch of salt and a teaspoon of oil. (The oil prevents the pasta sticking and the water slurping over.)

3   Keep it boiling as you gradually add the pasta (let long spaghetti coil itself into the pan).

4   Keep the water boiling briskly, uncovered. Stir from time to time with a fork to prevent the pasta sticking to the bottom.

5   Fresh pasta will take anything from 30 seconds to 2–3 minutes, depending on the shape. Dried pasta takes 6–15 minutes. Follow the times given on packets.

6   It is done when it is still chewy but soft, *al dente*: test a piece between your teeth. Alternatively, throw a strand at the wall. If it sticks, it's ready!

7   Pour it into a colander or sieve, or lift it out with a slotted spoon, getting rid of as much water as possible.

## NO-COOK SAUCES

*Grated cheese*   The simplest way of eating pasta is to add a tablespoon of oil or butter, mix it well so that each piece is glistening, add lots of freshly milled black pepper and 3–4 tablespoons of grated cheese. For added flavour, stir in a tablespoon of tomato purée or a clove of crushed garlic.

*Egg and grated cheese*   Break an egg into a bowl, add some pepper and a teaspoon of fresh chopped parsley, or ¼ teaspoon of dried. (Or you could use other herbs such as thyme, oregano, or sweet basil.) Beat well. When the pasta is cooked, drain it and mix in the bowl with the egg mixture. Sprinkle with 2–3 tablespoons of grated cheese and add more black pepper if required.

*Curd cheese and grated cheese*   In a bowl mix 4 tablespoons of curd cheese – you could use quark, ricotta or your own yoghurt cheese (see page 140). Mix using a fork with 2 tablespoons of grated hard cheese. Add salt, pepper and a pinch of nutmeg. Drain the cooked pasta and mix it with the cheese sauce. If necessary, add a little butter to moisten it.

*Yoghurt, walnut and grated cheese*   Mix 3 tablespoons of curd cheese with 2 tablespoons of yoghurt. Add salt and pepper and a tablespoon of chopped walnuts. Mix with the pasta, add a few small pieces of butter and 3–4 tablespoons of grated cheese.

*Yoghurt, egg and cheese*  Beat an egg and mix it with 4 table-spoons of plain yoghurt. When the pasta is cooked, drain it and mix with the sauce. Add plenty of black pepper and top with 4 tablespoons of grated cheese.

Any of the above would be even nicer with a sprinkling of chopped nuts such as pine-nuts, almonds, cashews, peanuts or walnuts, or seeds like sesame or sunflower. Add them plain or toasted (see page 75).

PESTO OR PISTOU SAUCE

The following recipe is for those who love garlic and the slightly unusual flavour of fresh basil. The sauce comes from Genoa where it is called *pesto* but it has become a part of the cooking of the South of France where it is known as *Pistou*.

> 6 fresh basil leaves
> 1 clove of garlic, chopped
> 3 tablespoons oil
> 1 tablespoon pine-nuts
> 2 tablespoons grated cheese

Your mortar and pestle will come in handy, but if you haven't got one, use a basin and the base of a bottle to crush the chopped garlic clove. Add the basil leaves, they are easier to crush if you chop them first with scissors. When the garlic and basil are mixed, add the pine-nuts and keep pounding until you have a fine paste. Add the oil. (In the Mediterranean area olive oil is used, but any good vegetable oil will do.) Beat the mixture well – you want the paste to absorb the oil and become a thick purée. Stir in the grated cheese, using a hard variety like Cheddar or Cheshire.

Drain the pasta and top with the sauce. Eat it with plenty of extra grated cheese and lots of black pepper.

GROWING FRESH BASIL

Fresh basil is an annual and it needs warmth and sun to make it grow. It isn't easy to find in this country unless you know a gardener or decide to grow your own in a pot on a sunny windowsill. You can buy it from garden centres or nurseries. Pinch out the flowers as they appear to encourage leaf growth.

The flavour is pronounced so you only need a little; it is marvellous with any dish or salad containing tomatoes. If you have to used dried basil, be very sparing.

*Parsley and nuts* You can make a sauce on the same lines as the recipe for *pesto*, using parsley instead of the basil and if you can't find pine-nuts, or you think they're too expensive, use almonds or walnuts, or even peanuts, instead.


## QUICK-COOK PASTA SAUCES

*Tomato* Put a pan or wok on a medium heat. When it is hot add a tablespoon of oil and some finely chopped garlic. Let it sizzle a moment but don't let it turn black or it will be bitter. (If you don't like garlic, use a chopped onion or leek instead and let it cook for 4–5 minutes till soft.) Add 3–4 ripe tomatoes cut in quarters. Cook the mixture over a high heat for 3 minutes; add some herbs such as a pinch of basil, oregano, marjoram, thyme, or mint; season with salt and pepper. Pour over the drained pasta and serve with grated cheese.

Instead of fresh tomatoes you could add half a can of Italian tomatoes – crush them in the pan with a spoon.

*Tomato with mushrooms* Heat a pan or wok. When it is hot add a tablespoon of oil and some finely chopped onion, a clove of garlic chopped and ½ teaspoon of chopped herbs such as parsley or thyme. Cook gently for five minutes.

Add 3–4 sliced mushrooms and let them cook for a few minutes until soft. Either stir in a couple of tomatoes roughly chopped or a tablespoon of tomato purée, and some pepper and cook uncovered for 5 minutes. Add salt to taste or a teaspoon of soy sauce. Serve with drained pasta and grated cheese.

You could add other ingredients to this basic sauce, in which case put them in when you have softened the onion. Here are some ideas: green or red pepper, sliced, seeds discarded; aubergine, chopped – add a little more oil as aubergine soaks it up; courgette, sliced; fennel – discard any tough outer leaves and slice thinly; chicory – wipe the outside leaves, then slice thinly.

When red or green peppers are expensive, it is worth having a drum of dried ones on hand – just add a tablespoon to your sauce. You can also buy dried mushrooms: follow the soaking instructions on the packet. You could consider adding a small packet of frozen peas, spinach or broccoli: defrost them in a little boiling water, drain and add to the sauce. Look out, too, for dried peas and onions – they are useful store standbys.

*Mushrooms in butter*   Heat about 2 tablespoons of butter in a pan or wok; when it is foaming add 100g (4oz) of chopped mushrooms. Cook quickly 3–4 minutes, season with salt, pepper and herbs such as thyme or parsley. Pour over the pasta and eat with grated cheese.

*Peas and mushrooms*   Bring a little water to the boil in a saucepan, add a tablespoon of butter and cook some frozen peas and two or three sliced mushrooms for 3–4 minutes. Drain and pour over the pasta; add salt, pepper and 2–3 tablespoons of grated cheese.

*Mushrooms and yoghurt*   Heat a pan or wok and add 2 table-spoons of butter or oil. When it is sizzling, add 100g (4oz) sliced mushrooms. Let them cook for a few minutes, remove from the heat and stir in a beaten egg, 2 tablespoons of yoghurt and a pinch of nutmeg. Serve on your drained pasta with 2–3 tablespoons of grated cheese.

*Spinach*   Follow the method in the above recipe but substitute 225g (8oz) spinach for the mushrooms, cooking the spinach first as on page 127 (or you could use a small packet of frozen spinach).

*Broccoli*   Cook 250g (8oz) broccoli, (see page 126). Drain and chop it. Mix it with 2–3 tablespoons of yoghurt and pour over the pasta. Sprinkle on 2–3 tablespoons of grated cheese.

*Sweet and sour pepper*   Heat a pan or wok and add a table-spoon of oil. When it is hot, add a chopped onion. While it is cooking, cut a green or red pepper into thin slices (discard the seeds), add it to the pan and cook gently until soft. Then stir in a tablespoon of tomato purée, a teaspoon of vinegar and ½ teaspoon of sugar. Season with salt, ½ teaspoon soy sauce, pepper and herbs such as sweet basil or thyme.

*Courgette and red pepper*   Heat a pan or wok, and when it is hot, add two tablespoons of oil. Add a chopped onion and let it soften for 3–4 minutes. Add a courgette cut in small pieces and a red pepper chopped, seeds discarded. Let them cook on a gentle heat for 15 minutes. Add salt or a teaspoon of soy sauce and some black pepper. Serve with plenty of grated cheese.

You could substitute an aubergine for the courgette.

*Red or green peppers with olives*   Heat a pan or wok. When it is hot add 2 tablespoons of oil and cook a chopped onion for 3–4 minutes until soft. Add a chopped red or green pepper (discard seeds), a pinch of oregano, salt and pepper. Let it cook on a gentle heat for 10–15 minutes. Add a tablespoon of black or green olives. Pour over the pasta and serve with grated cheese.

*Oil and garlic*   This has to be for garlic lovers but is too good to leave out! Heat 2 or 3 tablespoons of oil, and when it is hot add a clove of garlic cut in tiny pieces with, if you like, some chopped herbs such as parsley, thyme or oregano. Don't let the garlic brown, it should just sizzle and turn golden. Pour over your pasta and eat with plenty of grated cheese and freshly milled black pepper.

*For pasta sauces when you are in a great hurry* buy canned aubergines, courgettes, peppers, or ratatouille.

## WITH PULSE AND VEGETABLE DISHES

Pasta goes well with many of the dishes given in the chapters on 'Pulses' and 'Vegetables'. Or there's a very good brown lentil Bolognese sauce on page 93. The following dish made with chickpeas is called *tuoni e lampo*, which is a fair sample of Italian wit as translated it means:

THUNDER AND LIGHTNING

Heat a tablespoon of oil in a pan, add a chopped clove of garlic, ½ mug of cooked chickpeas (either your own or canned, see page 83) and heat them gently until hot. Mix them with your cooked and drained pasta, preferably small shapes such as shells; add 2–3 tablespoons of grated cheese or a sprinkling of sesame seeds or chopped nuts, and, if necessary, a little extra oil or a tablespoon of butter and some salt and pepper.

LEFTOVER SAUCES can be used next day on toast, as a filling for a jacket potato, stirred into a bowl of soup, served with an omelette or scrambled eggs, or as a pancake filling.

## LAYERED PASTA DISHES

These layered dishes are an incredibly cheap and efficient way of feeding several people and definitely not if you are just cooking for one! At first glance it may all seem daunting and complicated but having made one dish in this way, you will soon develop your speed and skills in devising others.

The dish consists of three layers. There is one of cooked pasta, another of a well-flavoured sauce made of vegetables or pulses, and then a layer of cheese which can either be a sauce, or simply grated or sliced cheese or spread curd cheese. First, a basic recipe, followed by other ideas for different sauces.

LASAGNE (4 servings)

    250–300 g (8–12 oz) lasagne
    1 tablespoon oil
    1 onion, chopped
    1 clove of garlic
    1 tablespoon tomato purée
    1 teaspoon sugar
    ½ teaspoon dried oregano (or use marjoram or basil)
    225 g (8 oz) tomatoes or use a medium can Italian tomatoes
    salt and pepper
    cheese sauce, either the uncooked or cooked version (see
       page 61)
    grated cheese

1  Cook the lasagne as on page 51 or use the ready-cooked variety.

2  Make the main sauce: heat the oil or fat in a small saucepan. When it is hot add the chopped onion and let it cook gently for about 5 minutes. Add the chopped garlic, tomato purée, sugar, herbs and sliced tomatoes. (If using canned tomatoes, crush them and keep the liquid for stock). Bring everything to the boil, cover, lower the heat and let it simmer for about 15 minutes.

3  While the tomato sauce is cooking, make the cheese layer (see page 61).

4  Use a shallow heatproof dish in which to assemble the dish. In the base put a layer of main sauce, followed by one of pasta and then a layer of cheese sauce. Repeat layers once more. Sprinkle over 3–4 tablespoons grated cheese, or lay thin slices of cheese on top.

5  Put the dish under a medium grill to brown the top for 5–10 minutes, or in the oven heated to Gas 5/375°F/190°C for 10–15 minutes. (You can also make these dishes ahead of time if you wish. They can then be reheated in the oven for 30–40 minutes.)

Additions to the basic sauce

*Mushrooms*   Add about 225g (8oz) sliced mushrooms after having softened the onion and let them cook for 2–3 minutes on a high heat. Continue with the basic recipe.

*Courgettes*   Add about 500g (1lb) sliced courgettes after softening the onion and let them cook for 2–3 minutes on a high heat. Continue with the basic recipe.

*Aubergines*   Cut 1–2 aubergines into small cubes. (If you have time, put them in a colander, sprinkle them with salt and leave for 30 minutes to drain their excess moisture. Pat them dry with kitchen paper.) Aubergines soak up oil, so add 2 more tablespoons after softening the onion in the basic recipe with the aubergine pieces and cook for several minutes, turning them over and over. Continue with the basic recipe.

*Green or red peppers*   Cut 1 or 2 green or red peppers into thin slices, discarding the seeds. Having softened the onion, add the strips of pepper and cook over a gentle heat for several minutes. Continue with the basic recipe.

*Pulses*    Add almost any kind of cooked beans to the cooked basic sauce and let it heat through for several minutes. Allow either 1 mug of cooked beans or a can.

*Spinach or broccoli sauce*    Instead of making a tomato and onion based sauce as in the previous ideas you could instead cook 1 kg (2 lbs) spinach or 500 g (1 lb) broccoli as on page 126–7. Drain well and chop finely, seasoning with salt and pepper and perhaps a pinch of nutmeg. Layer with pasta and a curd or cottage cheese sauce with perhaps 1–2 tablespoons of chopped nuts.

Cheese layer

There are several different methods in which you can make the cheese layer.

1    Use about 225 g (8 oz) curd or cottage cheese flavoured, if you like, with 2 tablespoons of chopped nuts such as walnuts, cashews, almonds or peanuts; a pinch of nutmeg and some salt and pepper, *or*

2    If the vegetable main sauce is quite moist, simply add grated or sliced cheese – you'll need about 150 g (6 oz), *or*

3    *Uncooked cheese sauce*    Mix about 225 g (8 oz) curd or cottage cheese with a beaten egg, add a pinch of nutmeg, one or 2 tablespoons of milk, perhaps ½ teaspoon of herbs such as parsley, thyme or oregano, and a little salt and pepper, *or*

4    *Cooked cheese sauce*    Put a mug of milk, or milk and water, into a small saucepan and 1 tablespoon of oil, butter or margarine. Add 2 tablespoons of wholemeal flour, either plain or self-raising. Bring to the boil over a medium heat, beating all the time with a whisk, fork or wooden spoon. As soon as the mixture begins to thicken, lower heat. Let it simmer for 2 minutes, to prevent the flour from tasting raw. Take off the heat, add salt, pepper and a pinch of nutmeg and stir in 3–4 tablespoons of grated cheese. If the sauce seems too thick, stir in a little more milk as flours do vary a little.

*Mustard with cheese sauce*    Mustard adds an interesting flavour to cheese sauces. Add a teaspoonful either to the uncooked version, or to the cooked stirring it in at the same time as the grated cheese.

*Wheatgerm and sesame seeds or chopped nuts* You can add interest to these dishes by topping them with a mixture of grated cheese, wheatgerm and either sesame seeds or chopped nuts.

#  PANCAKES

Pancakes are not just for Shrove Tuesday but are delicious at any time with savoury fillings. They are easy and quick to make and you can eat them right away or make a stack and keep them in the fridge. Once you've learnt the technique you'll be able to rustle them up with no trouble at all. Whether you decide to toss them or take the easy way out and turn them with a spatula is up to your sense of courage. To toss a pancake give the pan a quick flip to make the pancake turn a somersault – it doesn't have to hit the ceiling!

TO MAKE PANCAKES

1   Make the pancake batter (see page 64) and if there is time, let it stand for 30 minutes before you cook it as this enables the flour to swell and improves the pancakes.

2   Use a small frying pan; place it over a medium heat and when it is hot, smear it with oil or butter.

3   Pour about 2 tablespoons of batter into the pan and tilt it round so that the batter covers the base thinly. Dribble in a little more batter into any holes that occur.

4   Let the batter cook for 30–60 seconds until the surface is opaque and blisters begin to form.

5   Turn or toss it and cook the second side for about 20 seconds. Remove from pan.

If you're going to store the pancakes, it's worth interleaving them with strips of greaseproof paper to prevent them sticking together.

If you're going to eat them immediately, you simply put a filling down the centre, roll it up, sprinkle perhaps with some grated cheese or sesame seeds, and, if you like, brown under a hot grill for 2–3 minutes.

BATTER FOR PANCAKES (QUANTITIES FOR 3–4 PANCAKES)

Wholemeal flour makes very tasty pancakes and in Brittany and Russia buckwheat flour is used. It is rather expensive but you can buy it in small packets and it is an excellent source of the B vitamins. The flavour is quite strong and the pancakes won't be as light, so you might like to mix it half and half.

> 3 tablespoons flour either wholemeal (self-raising or plain will do), buckwheat or half and half mixture
> pinch salt
> 1 egg
> 7 tablespoons milk or a mixture of milk and water
> 1 teaspoon oil

Sieve the flour and salt into a bowl, the bran won't go through the mesh, but add it as well. If you haven't got a sieve, never mind, but sieving makes lighter pancakes. Make a hollow in the centre and break in the egg. Mix it and then gradually stir in the milk. Using a fork or whisk beat the batter vigorously for a minute or two. When you are ready to make the pancakes, add the teaspoon of oil and beat again for a couple of minutes. Cook as on page 63.

If you prefer you can add either a tablespoon of yoghurt, sour milk, buttermilk or milk-and-water instead of one of milk.

Fillings for pancakes

Fill your pancakes with one of the quick-cook sauces given in the pasta section on pages 56–8, or a sauce made with pulses such as those on pages 89–91, or a vegetable filling like ratatouille, on page 131. Or, use them in place of the lasagne in a layered dish topped with grated cheese or a cheese sauce (see page 59).

TORTILLAS (makes 4)

These Mexican pancakes are made with cornmeal without egg and are rolled out not poured. They are more complicated to make than ordinary pancakes but are a great way of feeding several people. You can fill them with almost any sort of sauce but they are nicest with something a bit spicy like the cheese and onion or chilli sauce fillings on pages 65–6.

4 tablespoons cornmeal
4 tablespoons wholemeal flour (self-raising or plain)
pinch salt
1 tablespoon oil
about 6 tablespoons warm water

Sieve the flours and salt into a bowl, adding the bran that remains in the sieve. Using a knife mix in the oil, followed by the water, which you should add gradually until you have a firm dough. (Flours vary, so it's not possible to be absolutely precise about the amount of water.) Put 1–2 tablespoons of flour on a board or table and some on your hands. Form the dough into a ball and knead it using the heel of your hand to push the dough away from you, turning and pushing and re-forming the ball. Knead until the dough feels pliant, 3–4 minutes. Set it aside to rest for 15 minutes – this will make it easier to roll. Then divide the dough into four, form each piece into a ball and roll them out on a floured board to make rounds about 15 cm (6 inches) in diameter.

Heat a frying pan over a medium heat and without adding any oil or grease, cook each pancake, turning it often until both sides are freckled.

Put the filling of your choice down the centre of each tortilla and fold them in half. Place them in a shallow heatproof dish and heat through under a moderate grill, or you can put them in an oven heated to Gas 5/375°F/190°C for about 15 minutes.

CHEESE AND ONION FILLING

Heat 1 tablespoon of oil in a frying pan; when it is hot add a chopped onion and cook until golden, about 5 minutes. Stir in 1 mug of grated cheese such as Cheddar or Cheshire, add ¼ teaspoon of ground cumin and the same of chilli powder, a pinch of salt and some pepper.

CHILLI SAUCE

> 1 tablespoon oil
> clove of garlic
> 1 onion, chopped
> 1 green or red pepper
> 1 tablespoon of tomato purée or 1 tomato, chopped
> pinch salt, pepper
> ¼ teaspoon oregano or marjoram
> ½–1 teaspoon chilli powder
> 1 mug cooked red kidney or aduki beans

Heat the oil in a pan or wok. When it is hot add the chopped onion and let it soften. Add the garlic – but don't let it blacken or it will be bitter – and then all the other ingredients. Mix well, cover the pan, lower the heat and cook for 10 minutes.

*Taco shells*   You can buy taco shells in packets. Use them like tortillas, following the instructions on the box.

# 🌿 RICE AND OTHER GRAINS 🌿

Everybody must have heard the praises of brown rice sung over those of white and few people can be unaware of how important grains are in Third World aid programmes, but they seem to have become an almost forgotten part of our own diet. We eat quite a lot of grain without being very aware of it: wheat is made into flour which is used in various products from bread to pasta, and cereals are the great standby of our national breakfast. But there are a host of grains to buy which are as simple to cook as rice (and all slightly higher in protein) and can be included in soups, mixed with pulses, made into salads or eaten with vegetable or egg dishes – in fact, in any of the ways in which we normally eat rice.

If you look on the shelves of a wholefood or health store, you will find a bewildering array of grains and it is easy to turn away and buy rice instead. Don't be put off but begin with those that are quickest to cook such as bulgar wheat, buckwheat, millet, cous-cous and cornmeal. Buy one sort at a time, gradually introducing all the different kinds, and you'll be amazed at how delicious and versatile they are. Once you're an expert you can try the whole grains of barley, oats, rye and wheat, but they take longer to cook and need to be soaked overnight.

Let's concentrate on the easy ones with a brief description of each first, followed by cooking times, methods and some recipe ideas.

### BULGAR WHEAT

This is also known as cracked wheat and is the quickest grain of all to cook because the whole wheat grain has already been boiled, dried and cracked. It can be cooked by any of the methods on page 69 but if you just want a quick base for a meal, do it like this: put ½ mug of bulgar wheat into a bowl, pour over ¾ mug of boiling water, add ¼ teaspoon of salt and 1 tablespoon of soy sauce. Stir. Cover the bowl and leave for 10–15 minutes. The grain will swell and absorb all the water.

### BUCKWHEAT

Buy the kind sold as roasted buckwheat. This is actually an outsider, because it doesn't come from wheat but from a polygonaceous plant similar to dock or rhubarb. It came to Europe from Russia and in recipes the cooked version is often called kasha. The flour is used to make pancakes as well as pasta. It is pricier than the other grains but is rich in both vitamin A and the B vitamins. It cooks in 20 minutes and has a rich, nutty flavour and chewy texture.

### COUS-COUS

Cous-cous is not quite as nutritious as other grain products because it is made from refined wheat. But its claim to fame is that it forms part of, and gives its name to, a magnificent North African dish which includes chickpeas and vegetables in a fiery sauce. There is a recipe on page 132 and you can cheat to improve the protein value of the dish by using buckwheat in its place.

### MILLET

Ignore cries of, 'This is for budgerigars.' Lucky budgerigars – millet contains all the necessary parts of protein, is very cheap, cooks quickly and is delicious, especially mixed with grated cheese.

### RICE

Brown rice really is better than white and its strong, nutty flavour will soon make white rice seem pallid in comparison.

## HOW TO COOK GRAINS

It's handy to have some cooked grains stored in the fridge: if you cook half a mugful at any one time you will have enough for two meals. Grains swell in cooking to three or four times their volume; they can be cooked quite simply in water, or fried for a few minutes in hot oil before the water is added, on their own or with onion or garlic, which brings out their flavour. Vegetables or pulses can be added to make a complete meal in the pan, and you can stir yoghurt, butter or grated cheese into the cooked dish, or chopped nuts, dried fruits or sesame seeds. Or you could try the Persian trick of mixing in a raw egg yolk.

The table below gives amount of liquid, cooking times and appropriate methods for half a mug of each grain:

| | water or stock | cooking time | method |
| --- | --- | --- | --- |
| Buckwheat | 1½ mugs | 20 minutes | 1–5 |
| Bulgar wheat or cracked wheat | ¾ mug | 10–15 minutes | quick, page 67 and 2–5 |
| Cornmeal | 1 mug | 20 minutes | page 71 |
| Cous-cous | 1 mug | 20 minutes | 1–5 |
| Millet | 1½ mugs | 25 minutes | 1–5 |
| Rice, brown | 1 mug | 40 minutes | 1–5 |
| Rice, white | 1 mug | 20 minutes | 1–5 |
| Wholegrains – barley, oats, wheat, rye | 1 mug | Soak overnight and cook by methods 1–5 for 1–1½ hours | |

*Method 1* Put grain and liquid into a pan, bring it to the boil. Add a pinch of salt and any one of the following: ½ teaspoon of yeast extract; 1 tablespoon of soy sauce; 1 teaspoon of miso. Stir with a fork, cover, lower the heat and cook for the appropriate time. Remove from the heat and leave covered for 10 minutes.

*Method 2* Heat 1 tablespoon of oil in the pan. When it is hot add the grain and cook over a medium heat for 3–4 minutes, stirring all the time. This method brings out the flavour of the grain. Pour in the liquid (being careful it doesn't splutter and burn you), a pinch of salt and any one of the following: ½ teaspoon yeast extract; 1 tablespoon of soy sauce; 1 teaspoon of miso. Stir with a fork until it boils, cover, lower the heat and cook for the appropriate time. Remove from the heat and leave covered for 10 minutes.

*Method 3*   Heat 1 tablespoon of oil in the pan. When it is hot add a chopped onion or clove of garlic and let it cook for a few minutes before stirring in the grain. Cook over a medium heat for 3–4 minutes, stirring constantly. Add the liquid (watch out, it can splutter), a pinch of salt and any one of the following: ½ teaspoon of yeast extract; 1 tablespoon soy sauce; 1 teaspoon miso. Stir with a fork until it boils, cover, lower the heat and cook for the appropriate time. Remove from the heat and leave covered for 10 minutes.

*Method 4*   As Method 3 but add any chopped vegetable when cooking the onion such as 2–3 tomatoes, some mushrooms, 1–2 carrots, a stick of celery, a leek, a green or red pepper, 1–2 courgettes, or what you will.

*Method 5*   As Method 3 but stir in ½ mug of any cooked or canned pulses after adding the liquid.

DISHES WITH GRAINS

Eat grains with any of the sauces in the pasta, pulse or vegetable sections. Have them with egg dishes or stirred into soups. Make them a base for salads or add them to stir-fried vegetables. Use them in burgers, see page 88 substituting cheese if you like for the pulses given in that recipe.


CORNMEAL

Cornmeal is made from maize. It features in the cooking of North America, Italy and southern France as well as being used in Mexico to make tortillas. Look out for stoneground cornmeal which contains all the nutrients of the grain. Cornmeal can be eaten as an accompaniment to dishes or used as a thickener for soups. Its flavour is bland so you can be quite generous with the seasoning. Because of its fine, flour-like texture, it would go lumpy if cooked by the methods on page 69, so try either of the following two methods.

COOKING CORNMEAL

*Method 1*  Bring 1 mug of water to the boil, add ¼ teaspoon of salt. Mix half a mug of cornmeal with enough cold water to form a paste. Take the pan off the heat and stir in the paste. Add some pepper and either 1 teaspoon of soy sauce or ½ teaspoon of paprika. Bring back to the boil, stirring, cover the pan and let it simmer for about 20 minutes or until all the liquid is absorbed.

*Method 2*  Bring 1 mug of water to the boil, add ¼ teaspoon of salt. Slowly add half a mug of cornmeal, letting it flow in a thin stream into the water, stirring constantly so that lumps do not form. Add seasonings and continue the cooking as in Method 1.

Eat the cornmeal with the addition of 2–3 tablespoons of grated cheese, 1 tablespoon of butter and perhaps a pinch of nutmeg.

*Fried or grilled cornmeal*  This is a great way of using up left-over cornmeal and is found in recipe books from Italy and France. Spread the cooked cornmeal on a plate or baking sheet and let it get quite cold – it's best left until the next day. Cut it into wedges: about 1 cm (½ inch) thick. Heat a frying pan and add 1 tablespoon of oil or butter. When it is hot, fry the wedges on both sides until golden, or put them under a hot grill, turning once.

Eat the wedges with lots of grated cheese or the hot chilli sauce given on page 66.

## MORE CEREALS

The following notes are to help you sort out some of the other cereal products available.

BARLEY

Most useful form is barley flakes which you can add to muesli. There is a recipe for barley water on page 152 using the flakes which contain all the nutrients of the grain, that have been processed out of the better known pearl barley. Barley is used extensively in brewing.

OATS

Widely available as flakes, rolled oats and oatmeal and most useful added in these forms to muesli; for making porridge, crumble or gratin toppings; or in biscuits and cakes. Quick-cook porridge oats, though handy, have lost nearly all their natural nutrients.

RYE

Flakes can be bought for adding to muesli or the whole grains added to salad. Rye flour is used to make a dark, textured loaf sold as pumpernickel. It is also used in America to make whiskey.

WHEAT

Wheat is used extensively in this country to make flour for bread, pasta, pastry, etc. Add wheatflakes to muesli and the whole grains to salads.

WHEATGERM

When white flour is made, the embryo or germ of the wheat is milled out of the grain. This contains everything that is needed in the grain to produce the new life of the wheat. It is sold quite cheaply and is an excellent means of adding nutrients to all sorts of dishes. It doesn't have to be cooked, so it can be mixed with cereal, used instead of breadcrumbs to top gratins, and mixed with crumble toppings or stuffings.

# NUTS AND SEEDS

Nuts make one of the most delicious types of burger, easy to put together and full of flavour. Seeds give a whole host of subtle flavouring when used as spices, they are also lovely toasted and eaten as a snack, or sprinkled over salads or with mueslis. Both chopped nuts and seeds can be added to gratin toppings, or mixed with cooked dishes of grains or pulses, as well as playing their more familiar part of being used in cakes and biscuits, sweets and icecream.

## NUTS

### ALMONDS

Used a lot in sweet making. They are ground and mixed with icing sugar to make marzipan, toasted with sugar until it caramelizes to make praline and used in macaroons and ratafias, as well as all kinds of confectionery. They also taste good in savoury dishes made with rice or grains, mixed with muesli or in salads, and with stir-fried vegetables. A spoonful or two ground and added to soup not only gives a beautiful flavour but also thickens it slightly. They are sold whole, flaked or ready-ground, and although quite expensive are a good buy as they contain more useful protein than any other nut.

### BRAZILS

These are lovely eaten as they are with fruit after a meal, or chop them and mix them with fruit to be stirred into yoghurt. Or add them to a mixed salad which contains oranges or apples.

## CASHEWS

Always sold ready shelled because the shell contains a toxin harmful to the skin. They are a little pricy but make delicious burgers, roasts or gratins, and go well with grains and cooked vegetables.

## CHESTNUTS

Wonderful roasted in their shells over a fire. They are tiresome to peel in quantity and that is probably why they are always sold in their skins. However, if you want to peel a few, it doesn't take long if you slit each one before immersing them in boiling water for a few minutes, when the skin will rub off. Chestnut purée in tubes and cans is imported from France, and is nice added to soups. Dried, peeled chestnuts can be found in some health shops and can be chopped and added to vegetable dishes.

## HAZELNUTS

Can actually be found growing wild in hedgerows but they are also cultivated extensively to be used in confectionery and sweet dishes. The flavour is pleasant in salads and breakfast cereals, and they make lovely savoury burgers and roasts.

## PEANUTS

The odd one out because they are not nuts but part of the pulse family. They are used to make a cooking oil which is sold as groundnut oil and are also known as monkey nuts. Peanut butter is an excellent food provided you make sure it does not contain hydrogenated oil which unfortunately destroys much of the goodness. Best suppliers are likely to be wholefood shops especially those who make their own. It isn't difficult to make peanut butter if you have an electric blender or processor – see page 75. Buy whole, raw peanuts, not the roasted or salted kind. Eat them on their own or with muesli, as part of salads, or made into burgers or gratins. They are cheap and very high in protein and go beautifully with dishes containing grains.

### PINE-NUTS OR PIGNOLIAS

These are expensive but are rich in protein and as their flavour is very distinctive you do not need to use vast quantities. They are used a great deal in Mediterranean cooking. If you can't get hold of them try using almonds, walnuts or even peanuts in their place. The simplest way to use pine-nuts is crushed and sprinkled on top of gratin dishes.

### WALNUTS

These slightly bitter nuts that look a little like tiny shrivelled brains go beautifully with cheese dishes, vegetables, or added to salads especially those containing apples or oranges. They also make delicious burgers or gratins.

### PREPARING NUTS FOR USE

The thin, papery skin that covers most nuts is edible but if you want to remove it you can do so by immersing the nuts in boiling water. Leave for 2–3 minutes after which the skin will rub off. Or you can toast them in a frying pan or wok, tossing them over a high heat – the skins will flake off and the nuts turn gold. Watch you don't burn them.

If you are using the oven, you can put a tray of nuts to toast for 10–15 minutes. Again, keep an eye on them to see they do not burn.

*To chop nuts*  Nuts can be chopped quite effectively using a mortar and pestle or you could use a bowl and a bottle. A small electric coffee grinder is a handy implement for this purpose.

### PEANUT BUTTER

Toast 1 mug of peanuts as above. Grind them in an electric blender or processor, gradually adding a little oil (2–3 table-spoons), preferably peanut or groundnut, to make a paste. If you like crunchy peanut butter add some coarsely ground peanuts to the mixture. Keep the butter in a jar in the fridge; if it separates, just stir it up.

Below are some basic recipes using nuts as the main ingredient.

NUT BURGERS (makes 2)

> 1 tablespoon oil
> 1 small onion or 1 leek, finely chopped
> 1 clove of garlic, optional
> ½ mug wheatgerm, breadcrumbs, cooked grain or mashed potato
> ¼ mug chopped or grated nuts such as almonds, walnuts, cashews, peanuts, or a mixture
> salt, pepper
> ¼ teaspoon dried herbs or spices, see below
> ½ tablespoon soy sauce or ¼ teaspoon of miso or yeast extract
> ½ tablespoon tomato purée (optional)
> egg or yoghurt
> 1–2 tablespoons wholemeal flour or wheatgerm mixed with sesame seeds for coating.

Heat the oil, add the chopped onion and let it cook over a medium heat for 3–4 minutes. Mix in all the other ingredients except the flour, using enough egg or yoghurt to make a firm but slightly moist mixture. Using wet hands to prevent the mixture sticking, form two flat, round cakes. Coat them with the flour or the mix of wheatgerm and sesame seeds. If possible set them aside for 20 minutes to firm up. Fry them on both sides in hot oil.

Vary the taste of these burgers by adding different flavours. Here are some ideas:

*Herbs*   Use whatever herbs you fancy such as parsley and thyme, oregano or marjoram, mint, coriander, or sweet basil.

*Spices*   Add a pinch of something spicy such as nutmeg, paprika, cayenne pepper, ground cumin, crushed coriander seeds, turmeric, or finely chopped root ginger. Fry the spice for a few minutes with the onion to bring out the flavour.

*Mushrooms*   Add a couple of finely chopped mushrooms to the mixture.

*Cheese*   Add 1 tablespoon of grated or curd cheese to the mixture. Or, divide the mixture into four pieces and make four flat cakes, sandwiching some cheese between each pair. The cheese will melt in the centre as you fry them.

*Tofu* Use tofu in the same way as cheese.

*Stuffed Vegetables* The mixture for Burgers can also be used to stuff vegetables, see page 134.

NUT LOAF OR GRATIN (serves 2–3)

If you want to feed more than one person you can use the burger mixture to make a loaf or gratin. Double the quantities and leave out the flour. As roasting will dry the mixture it is a good idea to add some liquid, perhaps in the form of a can of Italian tomatoes (crush them a little first) or ½ mug of stock or water. You can if you wish also add some cooked or canned pulses, 1–2 tablespoons per person.

Grease a loaf tin before adding the mixture. Sprinkle over some grated cheese, breadcrumbs or wheatgerm mixed with sesame seeds, and dribble a little oil over the top.

Cook for 30–40 minutes at Gas 4/350°F/180°C.

Note on making breadcrumbs

Use stale bread and grate it (or if you have a liquidizer or food processor use that). You can also use the crumbs left over from making toast.

SEEDS

A whole variety of seeds are used to add flavour to dishes and these include cumin and coriander, fennel and aniseed, dill and caraway. You can buy them either whole – crush them in mortar and pestle when you need them powdered – or already ground. Seeds can be used to make teas or tisanes; the method is on page 150.

Apart from those I have just mentioned there are several others which feature strongly in vegetarian cooking both to add flavour and texture and also because of their high protein content.

## SUNFLOWER AND PUMPKIN SEEDS

Delicious plain or toasted with muesli or salads, or as part of the topping for those dishes which you plan to brown under the grill or in the oven, or you can nibble them as a snack instead of crisps. To toast them heat a frying pan or wok and when it is hot add a handful of seeds. Toss them for a few minutes until they turn golden all over and remove immediately from the hot pan or they will blacken. Sprinkle a little salt over them.

## ALFALFA SEEDS

Very good for sprouting. The method is the same as for sprouting pulses (see page 95). They grow into thin threads about 4–5 cm (1½ – 2 inches) long and are delicious in salads or sandwiches.

## SESAME SEEDS

Perhaps the most useful of them all. They are used to make tahini, are lovely sprinkled over salads, with cooked vegetables, as part of toppings – either plain or toasted (toast them as for sunflower and pumpkin, they take no time at all). You can mix them with salt to make a tasty condiment called *gomasio*. Simply toast two tablespoons of sesame seeds and when they are golden, crush them to a powder in mortar and pestle (or grinder) and mix with 1 teaspoon salt. Use it to sprinkle on food at the table. Store in a dry jar.

# 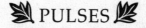 PULSES

Pulse is the not-very-inspiring group name for all those dried lentils and beans which form such an important part of vegetarian cooking. They are used in robust peasant dishes from all over the world, but their name of poor man's meat condemned them to the same fate as brown bread or flour. Or they are just a joke: the sight of a poor student and his pot of lentils has people roaring with laughter, as of course does their explosive reputation for causing excess wind and bloated stomachs. Lately, there have been dire warnings about certain beans being toxic, and then, of course, there is all that soaking and boiling before you can make anything of them. And horrid tales of boiling the beans for hours and hours only to find they are still not soft.

As a vegetarian, you won't of course allow yourself to be too influenced by all this gloom and scoffing but will rejoice in the marvellous versatility of beans. Cook them with grains; eat them with pasta; stuff vegetables; fill quiches and gratins; make soups and burgers; crush them into fillings for sandwiches; mix them with stir-fried vegetables; use them in salads, or sprout them.

The seemingly enormous variety isn't daunting because it doesn't take long to realize that although specific recipes state specific beans, you can break all the rules and use whatever you have on hand. To minimize the soaking and cooking problem, begin first with those that need no soaking which, being thin-skinned, are also the most digestible. Sample the canned versions of those that need soaking. Once you begin to feel your way around and understand how to use them in your cooking, soaking won't appear so arduous but just a question of remembering to do it.

Those harmful toxins present in some beans are easily dealt with by fast boiling for 10 minutes and if you are worried about remembering which are the culprits, simply boil all your beans in this way and forget the problem. To make sure your beans do soften, don't add salt or anything acid, like tomato or lemon, until the end of cooking time; never add bicarbonate of soda to soaking or cooking water as suggested in some recipes; it may soften them but it also destroys the food value.

As to wind and all that that implies, what can we do? Well, introduce pulses gradually into your diet to give your body a chance to adjust. Soft-skinned beans are the most easily digestible and can be made more so by a preliminary soaking. Certain herbs and spices are reputed to prevent flatulence and can be added to the cooking water. These are: bayleaf, aniseed, caraway, fennel, cumin or coriander. Some people suggest making a tea from aniseed, caraway and fennel either singly or mixed (see page 150) as a cure for flatulence. If you still have problems, make sure you rinse the beans thoroughly between each process. You can even bring the soaked beans to the boil and throw away this water after 5 minutes, before recommencing the cooking process in fresh water.

## UNSOAKED PULSES

### SPLIT RED LENTILS

Bright orange before cooking when they become a buff yellow purée. They can be eaten cooked quite simply as on page 82, or with rice, made into burgers, as a quiche filling or to stuff vegetables. A handful can be added to almost any soup to make it more satisfying and filling.

### SPLIT PEAS

Yellow or green and can be used as split red lentils or made into the traditional *pease pudding*. Cook ½ mugful of split peas as on page 82. While they are cooking, fry a chopped onion in 1 tablespoon of butter until it is golden. When the peas have formed a purée, after 30–40 minutes, stir in the onion, add a beaten egg and season with salt and pepper. The mixture is then steamed in a pudding basin, covered with a cloth tied with string (you could use foil instead). The basin is set over a pan of simmering water for about an hour. Or else break with tradition and put the mixture into a greased loaf tin or shallow oven dish and cook it in the oven Gas 4/350°F/180°C for 25–30 minutes.

## MUNG BEANS

Tiny, olive green beans with a sweet flavour which are excellent for sprouting (see page 95). Or cook them as described on page 82, flavouring them with a chopped clove of garlic, a little grated ginger and a pinch of cayenne pepper. They make an excellent Kicheri (see page 86) or a spread for sandwiches, and are good with salad or cooked with vegetables.

## CONTINENTAL LENTILS

They come in various sizes and colours – grey, green, brown or dark red. Unlike split lentils, they do not form a purée when cooked and as they absorb other flavours readily, they lend themselves to those recipes which in a meat diet specify mince, see the bolognese sauce on page 93. I especially like the brown or dark red lentils, the green and grey seem blander. You could use lentils as a base for a cottage pie, in layered pasta dishes or in moussaka, see page 93. They are good cooked with rice or in burgers. In fact, this is a most versatile bean, high in protein and especially useful because it needs no soaking.

## BLACK-EYED BEANS

Pale beige marked with a black outlined eye. Their colour becomes tinged with pink when they are cooked. The taste is pleasantly savoury. Use them in almost any of the recipes and they make an excellent substitute for any white beans in recipes you may come across elsewhere.

COOKING TIMES FOR BEANS THAT REQUIRE NO SOAKING

| | |
|---|---|
| Split red lentils | 20–30 minutes |
| Split peas | 30–45 minutes |
| Mung beans | 30–45 minutes |
| Continental lentils | 45–60 minutes |
| Black-eyed beans | 45–60 minutes |

These times are approximate as beans do vary. If you decide to soak any of these pulses, the cooking time will be shortened by about 10 minutes.

COOKING UNSOAKED BEANS

Beans swell during cooking. It is worth cooking half a mugful at any one time which should do for two or three meals; store covered in a fridge for up to six days.

First, wash the pulses in a bowl of cold water, rinse them and pick out any bits of grit or stone. Put them in a pan with double their volume of water, add a bayleaf or a generous pinch of one of the following seeds: aniseed, caraway, fennel, cumin or coriander. Don't add salt or anything acid like lemon or tomatoes at this point as these inhibit the softening process. Bring the pan to the boil, cover it, lower the heat and simmer for the stated cooking time. When they are soft, add a pinch of salt and, as their own flavour can be bland, now is the time to stir in some seasoning such as one of the following: 1 tablespoon soy sauce; a chopped onion or clove of garlic; a squeeze of lemon juice; ½ teaspoon of miso; ½ teaspoon of yeast extract; 1 teaspoon of tomato purée; or herbs, such as a pinch of oregano, thyme or parsley. Stir well and leave to infuse with a lid on for about 10 minutes. Any cooking liquid that remains can be used as stock.

You can eat these cooked pulses with any sort of grain, pasta, or with pitta or wholemeal bread. Or use them in the dishes outlined later in this section (pages 86 to 93).

If you want to eat them just as they are, a delicious trick which comes from Indian cooking is to fry a little chopped onion in a little hot oil and when it is soft, add ½ teaspoon of cumin or coriander seeds. As soon as they sizzle, tip them over the cooked pulses.

# PULSES WHICH NEED SOAKING

All these pulses have tough outer skins and need to be soaked before they are cooked which makes them more digestible. Planning ahead is anathema to some people and it can be infuriating to discover you should have done so if you want a meal in a hurry.

Solve this problem by trying out some of these pulses in their canned versions, and keep a can on two in stock. Once you have gained experience in preparing bean dishes, you will be less put off by soaking and cooking, especially as it will save you money. It really involves no great trouble, just a bit of forward-thinking. I suggest you always cook more than you need for one meal, so you will have something in hand for another day. Pulses keep for about six days, covered in a fridge.

### ADUKI BEANS

Small burgundy-red beans with a light sweet flavour. They cook very quickly and the stock is particularly wholesome. They make good burgers and feature in a dish called Red Rice (see page 87) and can be used in any of the bean dishes that follow, especially those which call for red kidney beans.

### CHICKPEAS

These have a soft texture and mild flavour and are used in dishes all over the Mediterranean and in Asia. They are used in hummus (see page 44) and cous-cous (see page 132); make a delicious garlicky soup (see page 100); and are good cooked with rice, or in dishes with tomato and vegetable like cour- gettes, aubergine, sweet peppers. Use them to make falafel (see page 92) or as a base for a salad, or make Thunder and Lightning (see page 59), or any of the bean dishes that follow on page 86–93.

### HARICOT BEANS, BUTTER BEANS, CANNELLINI

All white beans of varying sizes with bland, delicate flavours. Haricots come in the baked bean tins. Use in any of the recipes on pages 86–93 or in soups or salads.

RED KIDNEY BEANS

Used in the ever-faithful chilli sauces, they are delicious with
hot spices and make a good filling for tortillas (page 66). They
are pleasant in soups and salads and cooked with rice.

BLACK BEANS

Used a great deal in West Indian cooking. They can replace
red kidney beans or aduki beans in many recipes. There is a
famous Caribbean dish called Moors and Christians made
from cooked black beans and white rice. Cook as Red Rice (see
page 87) but add a chopped green pepper to the softened
onion and flavour the dish with ½ teaspoon of paprika or
chilli powder. If you use white rice, reduce the cooking time
to 20 minutes.

SOYA BEANS

The richest of all beans containing all the necessary protein
components, but as you will see from the table, they take an
inordinately long time to cook, and it is doubtful if any but the
most patient among us have the dedication to cook them
often.

Fortunately, all sorts of clever ways have been devised over
the centuries to release their goodness without causing the
cook too much trouble. For example,

*Soya flour* can be added to soups and sauces to increase their
protein value. Stir in 1–2 tablespoons, it contains no gluten so
has not the thickening or rising power of grain flours.

*Soya milk* is used by vegans instead of cow's milk. Watch out if
you add it to hot drinks: it may curdle but it won't affect the
flavour. Use it just like ordinary milk.

*Soya flakes or grits* are sold in some wholefood and health
shops and can be added to muesli or used in cooking. Different kinds have different cooking methods, so follow the
packet directions.

*TVP – Textured Vegetable Protein* is made from soya beans.
Although the producers wax lyrical about this, it is perhaps
more likely to appeal to those who miss meat and want
something that imitates it. If this is for you, you will find
packets with full cooking instructions. It is sold in wholefood

and health shops as well as some other shops and super-markets. Other soya bean products such as soy sauce, miso and tofu are discussed elsewhere in this book, see the Index.

SOAKING PULSES

There are two tried methods and the one you use will depend upon your temperament and lifestyle. I suggest you cook half a mugful at a time which will swell in soaking and cooking to give you sufficient for 2–3 meals.

First, wash the pulses and throw out any bits of grit or stones.

*Method 1* Put the beans into a pan, cover them generously with cold water and leave to soak for at least 8 hours (chick-peas should be soaked for 24).

*Method 2* Put the beans into a pan, cover with twice as much cold water, bring it to the boil and simmer for about 5 minutes. Turn off the heat and leave them to soak for 1 hour (chickpeas for 2–3 hours).

COOKING TIMES FOR SOAKED BEANS

| | |
|---|---|
| Aduki | 30 minutes |
| Black beans | 1 hour |
| Butter beans* | 1¼ hours |
| Cannellini beans | 1 hour |
| Chickpeas | 1–1¼ hours |
| Haricot beans | 1–1½ hours |
| Red kidney beans* | 1 hour |
| Soya beans | 3–4 hours |

COOKING SOAKED BEANS

Drain the soaked beans, rinse and put into a pan. Cover them with 2½ times the volume of water and add one of the following: a bayleaf, a generous pinch of aniseed, caraway,

---

*These beans contain toxins which are harmful, so make sure you boil them hard for at least 10 minutes when cooking them. You may find it simpler to make a habit of doing this when cooking all pulses.

fennel, cumin or coriander. Don't add salt or anything acid like lemon or tomato at this point as it inhibits the softening process. Bring the pan to the boil and, in the case of those beans asterisked, boil hard for 10 minutes. Lower the heat, cover the pan and simmer for the stated cooking time. If a layer of scum collects on top as it does with some kinds, remove it with a spoon. Beans vary and so do cooking times, old beans take longer than new. They are ready when they are soft.

At this point add some seasoning – a pinch of salt and one of the following: 1 tablespoon of soy sauce, a chopped onion or clove of garlic, a squeeze of lemon juice, ½ teaspoon of miso, ½ teaspoon of yeast extract, 1 teaspoon of tomato purée, or a generous pinch of herbs such as parsley, thyme or oregano.

The beans I have concentrated on are varieties which are easy to obtain and will provide you with a fair choice. There are a great many other kinds which you will see in wholefood, health shops and Asian stores. Once you have become an expert in cooking with them, you will find it immensely satisfying to search out recipes and experiment with some of the many other possibilities.

## RECIPES FOR DISHES WITH PULSES

You can make a complete meal in a pot using rice, pulses and vegetables. In India this sort of dish is called Kicheri (the word from which our own kedgeree is derived). It really means a sort of hotch-potch. The following recipe uses the kind of beans that need no soaking and beans, rice and vegetables are all cooked together.

KICHERI (2 servings)

> 4 tablespoons mung beans; or split red lentils; or split peas; or continental lentils; or black-eyed beans
> 4 tablespoons brown rice
> 1 onion or 1 clove garlic, chopped
> thin slice root ginger, grated, or pinch ground ginger
> 1 potato, unpeeled and chopped
> 2 carrots, sliced
> 1 tablespoon oil

    1 mug water
    1 tablespoon soy sauce
    squeeze lemon juice
    pinch salt
    1 tomato sliced

Put all the ingredients in the pot except the lemon juice, salt and tomato. Bring to the boil, stir well, cover the pot and simmer for 40 minutes. Add lemon juice, salt and tomato. Turn off the heat and leave covered for 10 minutes. Continental lentils and black-eyed beans may take a little longer. If, after 40 minutes, they still seem a little hard, add a little more water if necessary and continue the cooking for a further 10 minutes or so. You can of course adapt this recipe to whatever vegetables you have on hand. If you want it spicier, add a pinch of cumin and ½ teaspoon of paprika.

COOKED PULSES WITH RICE AND OTHER GRAINS

Pulses can be added to almost any kind of grain to make a satisfying meal. One way to do this is to add cooked or canned pulses to the uncooked grain. In the section on grains you will find the method explained together with time for cooking the different grains. Use ½ mug of cooked pulses with the same amount of uncooked grain.

Aduki beans make a beautiful dish called red rice. The method is the same as for cooking any pulse with a grain but I am giving the recipe below as a guide to this dish and the general method.

RED RICE (2 servings)

    1 tablespoon oil
    1 onion, chopped
    1 clove garlic, chopped
    1 teaspoon sesame seeds
    ½ teaspoon cumin
    ½ mug uncooked brown rice
    ½ mug cooked or canned aduki beans
    pinch cayenne pepper or, for a milder flavour, ½ teaspoon
        paprika
    1 mug water
    pinch salt

Heat the oil in a pan. Add the chopped onion and cook for 2–3 minutes; add the chopped garlic, sesame seeds and cumin and let them just sizzle. Stir in the rice and mix until every grain is coated. Add the aduki beans, and cayenne or paprika. Pour in the water, bring to the boil and add the salt. Put on the lid, lower the heat and simmer for 40 minutes. Remove from the heat and leave for 10 minutes before eating.

*Red rice pie*    You can make this into a filling pie by putting the cooked beans and rice into a heatproof dish and adding a topping of a mixture of grated cheese and wheatgerm, with perhaps a few sesame seeds or chopped nuts sprinkled over. Put it under a hot grill to brown.

Or make a topping of mashed potato and brown it in the same way.

You can finish off any combined dish of pulses and grains in this manner.

### BEAN BURGERS

Almost any kind of cooked pulse can be made into delicious burgers. Use your own supply or those from a can.

> 4 tablespoons any cooked or canned pulses
> 3 tablespoons wheatgerm; or cooked grain; or oatmeal; or breadcrumbs
> 1 tablespoon finely chopped onion or garlic
> 1 teaspoon tomato purée
> 1 teaspoon soy sauce or ½ teaspoon miso
> salt, pepper
> 1 tablespoon yoghurt or a beaten egg
> 1–2 tablespoons wholemeal flour

Mash the beans and mix with all the other ingredients except the flour. With damp hands to prevent the mixture sticking form two round burgers. Coat them evenly on both sides in the flour. Set them aside for 20 minutes to firm up. Fry on both sides in a little hot oil.

You can add 1 tablespoon of grated cheese to the mixture if you like, or use curd cheese or tofu.

There are masses of ways to add cooked beans to vegetables

and below are some ideas to start you inventing. All these dishes could be eaten with pitta or wholemeal bread, on toast or with any sort of cooked grain or pasta. Or eat them topped with grated cheese, or incorporate them in an egg dish (see chapter on Eggs). You can use your own prepared beans or those from a can.

### BEANS WITH MUSHROOMS AND YOGHURT

> 100 g (4 oz) mushrooms, sliced
> 1 tablespoon butter or oil
> salt, pepper
> nutmeg
> ½ mug cooked beans
> squeeze lemon juice
> 2 tablespoons yoghurt

Heat the butter or oil in a wok or pan and add the sliced mushrooms. Stir-fry them for 3–4 minutes, add salt, pepper, a pinch of nutmeg and the cooked beans. Toss them over a high heat until they are hot through, add the lemon juice and yoghurt and eat at once.

### BEANS WITH TOMATOES

> 1 tablespoon oil
> 1 onion, finely chopped
> 1 carrot or ½ green pepper, chopped
> clove garlic, chopped
> pepper, salt
> pinch thyme, parsley, oregano, or sage
> ½ mug cooked beans
> 2 chopped tomatoes

Heat the oil in a wok or pan, add the onion and stir-fry for a few minutes, add the chopped carrot or green pepper and continue stir-frying for 3–4 minutes before adding garlic, salt, pepper, herbs and the cooked beans. Mix well and add the chopped tomato. Put on the lid and simmer gently for 5 minutes.

### BEANS WITH APPLE

    1 tablespoon oil or butter
    1 apple, chopped unpeeled
    ½ mug cooked beans
    1 teaspoon brown sugar or ½ teaspoon honey
    salt, pepper

Heat the oil or butter in a wok or pan, add the chopped apple
and let it cook gently for a few minutes. Stir in the cooked
beans, sugar, salt and pepper. Cook covered until hot for
about 5 minutes.

### BEANS WITH MUSTARD

    1 tablespoon oil or butter
    1 onion or 1 leek chopped
    1 teaspoon made mustard
    1 tablespoon tomato purée
    1 teaspoon brown sugar or ½ teaspoon honey
    ½ mug cooked beans
    ½ tablespoon soy sauce
    pepper
    little stock or water

Heat the oil or butter in a wok or pan, add the chopped onion
and stir-fry for a few minutes. Add mustard, tomato purée,
sugar, cooked beans, soy sauce and a little pepper. Cook over
a gentle heat, adding a very little water or stock if necessary,
until it is hot through.

### BEANS À LA PROVENÇALE

The original recipe is for chickpeas but you could use any
white bean. It also states saffron which has an elusive flavour
all its own and colours the dish a subtle yellow. Saffron is
expensive, so instead I use turmeric which has its own special
taste and golden colour. One day when you feel very rich, try
it with a few strands of saffron.

    1 tablespoon oil
    2 tomatoes, chopped
    1 clove garlic, chopped

sprig of fresh parsley, or ½ teaspoon dried
½ teaspoon turmeric
½ mug cooked chickpeas or any white bean
salt, black pepper

Heat the oil in a wok or pan and cook the chopped tomatoes
and the garlic for a few minutes – don't let the garlic blacken
or it will be bitter. (If you don't like garlic, use a chopped
onion or leek instead.) Add the parsley and turmeric and stir
in the cooked beans. Season with salt and pepper. Cover and
simmer for about 5 minutes.

### BEANS COOKED WITH ASSORTED VEGETABLES

Use any sort of vegetable you have on hand in this dish such
as mushrooms, peppers, courgettes, aubergines, leeks,
swede, fennel, cabbage, Chinese leaves, what you will. The
basic method remains the same. Heat your wok or pan, add 1
tablespoon of oil and soften a chopped onion. Add one or two
other chopped vegetables, more if you wish, and stir-fry for a
few minutes before stirring in half a mug of any cooked beans.
Flavour with 1 tablespoon of soy sauce or ½ teaspoon of miso,
perhaps 1 tablespoon of tomato purée, salt, pepper and ½
teaspoon of herbs or spices. Let it all cook gently over a low
heat, covered, for 5–10 minutes.

### Gratin toppings added to bean and vegetable dishes

If you want to make an even more filling dish, put the cooked
beans and vegetables from any of the above recipes into a
heatproof dish and add a topping. This can be grated cheese
alone or mixed with wheatgerm or breadcrumbs; or wheatgerm mixed with sesame seeds; or perhaps breadcrumbs with
a sprinkling of chopped nuts. Dribble a little oil over the top
and put under a hot grill to brown for a few minutes, or heat
in the oven Gas 5/375°F/190°C for 10–15 minutes.

### COCIDO

This is a Spanish method of cooking vegetables with beans,
usually with meat, to make a sort of stew. It can be adapted to
make a good vegetarian dish. The beans are half cooked
before the rest of the ingredients are added. Chickpeas would

normally be used in Spain but you could substitute any other sort of white bean. The method is as follows.

Prepare half a mug of chickpeas or other white beans as described in the method on page 85. Half-way through the cooking time add a selection of chopped vegetables (one or more of any of the following: carrot, leek, turnip, cabbage, potato, green pepper, courgette) plus a chopped onion and a clove of garlic. Add 1 teaspoon of paprika, a bayleaf, a pinch of thyme and parsley, salt and pepper, and stir in 1 tablespoon of oil. Continue cooking until the beans and vegetables are soft, adding a little more water if necessary.

### FALAFEL-CHICKPEA BURGERS

On the streets of the Middle East they sell deep-fried balls made from chickpeas called falafel, just like hot chestnuts are sometimes sold in winter here. Not perhaps very practical to make, as deep-frying is heavy on the oil, but you can make a delicious sort of burger with similar ingredients.

> ½ teaspoon coriander
> ½ teaspoon cumin
> ½ teaspoon chilli powder
> 1 mug cooked chickpeas
> small onion very finely chopped
> clove of garlic, chopped
> salt, pepper
> squeeze lemon juice
> 1 tablespoon yoghurt
> 1–2 tablespoons wholemeal flour

Crush the coriander and cumin with the chilli powder and the chickpeas, using a mortar and pestle, or a bowl with perhaps a wooden spoon or the base of a bottle.

Mix in the onion, garlic, salt, pepper and lemon juice and enough yoghurt to bind the mixture. Dampen your hands and form two flat burgers. Put the flour on a board and coat each burger on both sides. Set aside if possible for about 20 minutes to firm up. Fry in hot oil until golden on both sides.

The original recipe calls for fresh coriander leaves, but as you need so very little, you can use the seeds instead which give a sweeter flavour.

BROWN LENTIL BOLOGNESE SAUCE

You can of course use any other cooked bean you may have, but brown lentils are particularly good done this way.

2 tablespoons oil
1 onion or leek, chopped
1 clove of garlic, chopped
2 carrots or ½ green or red pepper, chopped
3 or 4 mushrooms
1 tablespoon tomato purée
½ can Italian tomatoes or 3–4 fresh
½ teaspoon oregano and thyme
salt, pepper
½ mug cooked brown lentils or other bean
1 tablespoon soy sauce

Heat the oil in a pan or wok and add the onion or leek. Cook for 3–4 minutes, add the garlic, the carrots or pepper, cook for 2–3 minutes, stirring without letting the garlic blacken. Add the mushrooms and stir-fry everything for a moment or two. Stir in the tomato purée and mix well before adding the tomatoes. Stir over the heat and add herbs, salt and pepper, the cooked beans and soy sauce. Simmer the sauce, covered, for about 15 minutes.

Eat this sauce with spaghetti or any other pasta, with rice or a cooked grain. It can be used as a base for a *cottage pie*: in this case prepare some mashed potato, pour the cooked sauce into a heatproof dish, top with the potato and brown under a hot grill for a few minutes. You can add a little butter or grated cheese to the potato topping if you wish.

This bolognese sauce could be used as one of the layers in a lasagne dish (see page 59) or in the following recipe.

MOUSSAKA

This is another good standby for feeding friends. Use the bolognese sauce above but double the quantities.

500 g (1 lb) aubergines
2–3 tablespoons oil
4–5 tablespoons grated cheese
2 tablespoons wheatgerm
1 tablespoon sesame seeds

Slice the unpeeled aubergine about ½ cm (¼ inch) thick. Sprinkle the slices with salt and set aside to drain excess moisture for about 30 minutes. You could make the bolognese sauce during this time.

Wipe the aubergine slices with a piece of kitchen paper. Heat the oil in a wok or pan and fry the slices on both sides until they soften – about 10 minutes in all.

Grease a heatproof dish with a little oil or butter and cover the base with half the aubergine slices. Pour over the bolognese sauce and top with remaining aubergine. Sprinkle with the grated cheese, wheatgerm and sesame seeds and dribble over a little oil. Brown under a hot grill.

If aubergines are unobtainable or expensive, use potatoes instead. Boil 3–4 medium potatoes in their skins (see page 118) until soft, slice them and use as described above.

This dish can be made more elaborate and filling by topping with a cheese sauce (see page 61). If you make the moussaka ahead of time heat it in an oven Gas 5/375°F/190°C for about 40 minutes.

USING PULSES IN OTHER DISHES

You will find pulses mentioned in other sections in this book: as spreads on page 44, with pasta dishes page 58, with rice and other grains page 70, in soups page 98, with eggs page 106, in salads page 114, as fillings for potatoes page 119 and with vegetables pages 129 and 135.

## BEANSPROUTS

Almost any kind of bean, or indeed grain or seed, can be sprouted with the exception of split peas or lentils or a grain which has been hulled. Use those bought from wholefood or health shops *not* the ones sold by seed merchants. The most commonly used are mung beans and as they sprout readily are perhaps the best for starters. You eat the bean and the sprout thus obtaining all the goodness with little effort.

METHOD OF SPROUTING

You need a wide-mouthed 1-litre (2-pint) glass jar, a piece of muslin, cheesecloth or J-cloth to cover the top and a rubber band with which to secure it.

Wash 2 tablespoons of beans in a sieve under running cold water before putting them to soak in the jar covered with water for about 8 hours. Rinse them again until the water runs clear and return them to the jar. Cover the top with the cloth, securing it with the rubber band. Lay the jar on its side to drain out any excess water. The beans must be moist but not swimming or they will go mouldy. Twice or three times a day, fill the jar through the cloth with water, and drain it away by laying the jar on its side. There is no need to keep the jar in the dark, but it is best if it is kept somewhere warm. After 3–4 days the beans will have sprouted pale, cream tendrils about 5–8 cm (2–3 inches) long and will fill the jar. Rinse them and keep them covered in a bowl in the fridge. They will stay fresh for 4–5 days, plenty of time in which to sprout a second batch.

Beansprouts are lovely with sandwiches, in salads or stir-fried.

# 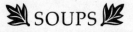 SOUPS

Home-made soups are so much nicer than canned or packet soups that having made a few you will never again be able to take the others seriously. There's not a lot more to it than throwing the ingredients into a pot, adding something tasty like herbs or spices, setting it to simmer for half an hour or so, when all the goodness will have been released, and then falling to and eating it with perhaps a thick chunk of bread and a sprinkling of grated cheese.

It's very easy to be inventive with this type of cooking, so try a few of my ideas and then go on to produce your own soup kitchen.

## STOCK

Soups made without meat or fish stocks need plenty of seasoning. You can make vegetable stock by boiling up vegetables, using peelings and bits of outer vegetable leaves, plus an onion; cover with water and simmer the whole lot for about 20 minutes, season with salt and pepper. Strain through a sieve or colander and keep the resulting liquid in a fridge for not more than 2–3 days. Save any liquid left over from cooking vegetables, especially potatoes, to use as stock; if you have any liquid from cooking pulses, this is also good, especially from white beans or aduki beans though some dark beans give a rather bitter-tasting stock. If you have no stock, don't worry, you will just need to make sure you add sufficient flavourings and seasoning.

## BASIC SOUP

There are hundreds and hundreds of recipes for making soups, but master the basic method and all the rest will follow.

The following quantities will give you 2–3 helpings.

2 tablespoons oil or butter
1 onion
500 g (1 lb) vegetables – see below for suggestions
clove of garlic, optional
1 tablespoon tomato purée; or 1 tablespoon soy sauce; or
    1 teaspoon yeast extract; or 1 teaspoon miso
bayleaf and ½ teaspoon of herbs and/or spices
1 tablespoon flour; or 1 tablespoon cornmeal; or 1 table-
    spoon ground almonds – optional thickening agents
3–4 mugs water or stock
salt, pepper

Heat the oil or butter in a large pan and add the chopped
onion and whatever vegetable you are using, also chopped.
Give it a good stir and cover the pan. Cook over a medium
heat for about 10 minutes. This sweating process allows the
vegetables to release their juice and flavour. Take off the lid,
add the chopped garlic and the flavouring you are using,
tomato purée or whatever. Stir the vegetables to make sure
none are stuck to the bottom. Add the bayleaf and herbs
(perhaps thyme, parsley or oregano) and/or the spices
(crushed coriander, cumin or fennel for example). Let them
cook for a minute or two. If using flour as a thickening agent,
stir it in now and mix well. Cook for a couple of minutes,
before gradually pouring in the water or stock. Bring to the
boil and add the salt and pepper. Cover the pan, reduce the
heat and let it simmer for about 30 minutes. Taste and add
more seasoning if necessary. If you are using cornmeal or
almonds to thicken the soup, now is the time. Mix the cornmeal with water to form a thin paste before stirring it into the
soup; or simply stir in the ground almonds.

Ideas for vegetable soups

You can make your soups using just one sort of vegetable, or
use two or three or more different kinds. Below are some
suggestions.

Potato with carrot and leek, flavoured with parsley or mint
Shredded cabbage with tomatoes (or use canned tomatoes
    using the liquid as part of the stock)
Carrots with onion, flavour with nutmeg and parsley

Mushrooms with thyme (use about 225 g [8 oz])
Tomato, flavoured with oregano or basil
Spinach with leeks, flavoured with nutmeg
Watercress and potato
Canned sweetcorn with tomato and a green or red pepper
Chestnut – make a base with onion, carrot and potato and stir
 in a can of chestnut purée, before adding the liquid

To make soups more filling

*Grains or Pasta* Add a handful to any soup. These can be cooked already, or if uncooked, make sure you allow enough time for them to soften.

*Pulses* The longer-cooking pulses are best added already cooked, either whole or crushed.

However, the quicker-cooking kinds like red split lentils, split peas and mung beans can be added raw. Put in about a handful, allowing an extra mug of liquid and make sure you don't add any salt or acid like lemon juice or tomato until near the end of cooking time.

*Cheese* Either grated or sliced, cheese is lovely with soup, making it thicker as well as tastier. Curd cheese, cottage cheese or yoghurt are also great additions.

*Bread or toast* Both are good broken up and added to soup. The French brown bread in the oven and put it into the soup bowl before pouring over the soup.

*Aioli or rouille* Add a spoonful or two of either of these pungent sauces to your soup or spread on toast and dunk it.

*Aioli* is a mayonnaise flavoured with garlic. You can either add a clove of chopped garlic to a ready-made mayonnaise or make your own. First, crush a clove of garlic in a mortar and make a mayonnaise as described on page 115.

*Rouille* is made like aioli but crush a whole hot chilli as well as the garlic, or use ½ teaspoon of cayenne pepper, before continuing with the mayonnaise. The name means rust-red, so to make the sauce redder, add ½ teaspoon of tomato purée.

*Pistou*   Another lovely soup addition. Follow the recipe on page 55 but omit the nuts.

*Garlic and herb bread*   Delicious with soup, and well worth making when serving soup to several people. Cut a french stick (some french sticks are made with wholemeal flour) into slices about 2.5 cm (1 inch) thick. Mix about 50 g (2 oz) butter with a clove of chopped garlic or 1 teaspoon of mixed herbs such as thyme and oregano. Spread this butter between the slices. Wrap the loaf loosely in foil and put it into the oven Gas 6/400°F/200°C for about 10 minutes.

Below are a few recipes for some special soups which don't exactly follow the basic method but are just as simple and worth making.

FRENCH ONION SOUP (2 servings)

> 500 g (1 lb) onions
> 2 tablespoons oil or butter
> 1 teaspoon sugar
> 3 mugs stock or water flavoured with either 1 tablespoon
>     tomato purée or soy sauce; or 1 teaspoon miso or yeast
>     extract
> salt, pepper
> toast and grated cheese

Peel the onions and cut into thin slices. Heat the oil, or butter, add the onions and sugar and mix well. The sugar helps to brown the onions. Cook over a low heat until the onions are soft and brown. Add stock or water with chosen flavouring, salt and pepper. Simmer 15 minutes. Pour into your bowl, top with the toast and grated cheese and, if you like, put under a hot grill to brown and bubble.

PEANUT BUTTER SOUP (2 servings)

> 1 tablespoon oil
> 1 onion
> 1 carrot
> 1 tablespoon tomato purée
> bayleaf, ½ teaspoon thyme
> 1 tablespoon soy sauce
> 2 mugs stock or water
> pinch salt
> 4 tablespoons peanut butter
> 2 tablespoons milk
> squeeze of lemon juice
> 1 teaspoon sesame seeds – optional

Heat the oil in a pan and add the chopped onion and carrot, cook them covered over a medium heat for 10 minutes. Stir in the tomato purée, add bayleaf, thyme and soy sauce. Mix well, pour in the stock and add salt. Bring to the boil, lower the heat and cook covered for 20 minutes. Mix the peanut butter with the milk and add to the pan off the heat. Add lemon juice. Bring just to boiling point and serve.

CHICKPEA SOUP (2 servings)

> 1 tablespoon oil
> 2 tomatoes, chopped
> 2 leeks, chopped
> 2 cloves of garlic, chopped
> 1 mug cooked chickpeas (or 1 can)
> 3 mugs water or stock
> salt, pepper

Heat the oil in a pan and cook the tomatoes and leeks over a medium heat, stirring all the time, until the leeks just begin to brown, and add the garlic.

Mash the chickpeas and add; pour over the water. Bring to the boil and simmer, covered, for about 15 minutes. Add salt and pepper to taste.

This soup is delicious with cubes of bread fried until brown in a tablespoon of oil.

AIGO-BOULIDO (1 serving)

This soup is made in Provence and the Languedoc and is said to be a restorer after a heavy night. It is simplicity itself to make but is only for those who like garlic.

> 1 mug water
> 2 cloves garlic
> 4 or 5 fresh sage leaves or ½ teaspoon dried
> salt, pepper
> 1 egg yolk (see page 116) or 1 tablespoon small pasta
> bread and grated cheese

Put water, peeled and crushed garlic and sage into a pan. Bring to the boil and season with salt and pepper. Simmer for 15 minutes. Remove the sage leaves. The soup is thickened by adding either an egg yolk or some pasta. If using the egg, to prevent it scrambling take the pan off the heat, stir in the yolk and serve immediately. If using pasta, add it to the pan and simmer until it is soft (10–12 minutes). If you have no small pasta shapes, you could break up some spaghetti.

Put a slice of bread, topped with grated cheese into a bowl and pour over the soup.

CABBAGE SOUP (4 servings)

A hearty soup to serve to friends on a cold winter's day.

> 1 cabbage about 1 kilo (2lb)
> 2 carrots
> 2 turnips
> 2 leeks
> 1 clove garlic
> 1 onion
> 5 potatoes
> 1 can Italian tomatoes
> 6 mugs water
> 2 tablespoons soy sauce
> salt, pepper
> 1 teaspoon herbs – thyme, oregano
> bayleaf

Slice all the vegetables and shred the cabbage. Put in a pan with all the other ingredients. Bring to the boil, cover, lower the heat and simmer for 1 hour. Serve with toast topped with grated cheese in the bottom of each bowl.

Two cold soups for summer:

CUCUMBER SOUP (1 serving)

>     1 tablespoon raisins
>     4 tablespoons cold water
>     1 tablespoon milk
>     4 tablespoons yogurt
>     1 tablespoon chopped peanuts
>     ¼ cucumber, peeled and cut in small pieces
>     1 clove of garlic, chopped
>     salt, pepper

Put all the ingredients into a bowl and put in the fridge to chill.

TOMATO SOUP (1 serving)

>     4 tablespoons yoghurt
>     1 tablespoon oil
>     squeeze lemon juice
>     4 tablespoons tomato juice, or use the liquid from canned
>        tomatoes
>     salt, pepper
>     ¼ teaspoon of marjoram, thyme, or basil

Mix the yoghurt with the oil, add lemon juice, tomato juice, salt, pepper and herbs. Chill in the fridge.

#  EGGS

Eggs provide just about our most compatible protein so they are a marvellous foil to all sorts of other foods such as potatoes and vegetables, grains and pulses, nuts and seeds. However, eat them in moderation because like all things which seem perfect – they have their shortcomings: too many may constipate you and the yolks are high in cholesterol. If you are upset by the miseries of battery farming, go for free-range eggs.

Below are ways of cooking eggs with some ideas and variations.

BOILED EGG

Eggs used straight from the fridge are likely to crack, so try piercing a hole in one end with a needle. You can put the egg into cold or boiling water, start timing when the water plus egg begins to bubble. Allow 3½ minutes for a runny egg; 4 minutes for a firm white and runny yolk; 5 minutes for a firm egg. Very fresh farm eggs will take an extra ½ minute.

*Hardboiled egg*   Cook as above for 9 minutes. Remove the egg from the pan immediately, crack the shell all over and put it into a bowl of cold water. This prevents a black rim forming round the yolk.

CODDLED EGG

This produces a more digestible egg than boiling. You boil the water, add the egg, remove from the heat and leave for 5 minutes.

POACHED EGG

Some people insist that it is not worth poaching eggs unless they are no more than two or three days old.

If you are lucky enough to get them this fresh, it is true you will produce a superior poached egg. Older eggs go a bit straggly but don't be dismayed, it is still a good, quick way of doing an egg.

Half fill a frying pan with water and bring it to the boil. Lower the heat and pull the pan half off the burner, so that only one side of the water is agitating. Break the egg on to a saucer or into a cup and slide it into the slightly bubbling water; the egg should hold its shape. Cover the pan and let the egg set, about 4 minutes. If the water continues to bubble fiercely, which is likely to happen on an electric burner, remove the pan completely from the heat.

Poached eggs can be eaten on toast, or topping a toasted or fried sandwich; as buck rarebit (see page 47), with spinach (see page 130) or with almost any pulse, grain or vegetable dish which you feel needs an extra fillip.

### EGGS BAKED OR STEAMED IN A COCOTTE

These small pots in which eggs are cooked either individually or in pairs can be found in specialist kitchen shops. They are made of heatproof porcelain or earthenware. The basic methods are as follows:

*On top of the stove* Put a teaspoon of oil, butter or margarine into the cocotte pot and stand it in a saucepan filled with water to reach half-way up the side of the cocotte. Bring the water to the boil, break 1 (or 2) egg(s) into the pot. Lower heat, cover the pan and leave 4–5 minutes for the egg(s) to set.

*In the oven* This is a useful method if you are cooking several eggs at once, or are already using the oven. Heat the oven to Gas 5/375°F/190)°C. Put a baking sheet in the oven on which you stand the cocotte pot(s) with their teaspoon of oil, butter or margarine. Let the oil or fat get hot, 3–4 minutes, break in the egg(s) and cook them in the oven until set, 6–8 minutes. You can if you wish break two eggs into each pot.

Different flavours can be added, the method is to put a spoonful or two of what you fancy on top of the oil or fat, break in the eggs and cook as above.

Some suggestions for flavourings

Yoghurt either on its own or with a chopped mushroom or two

Curd or cottage cheese

Sprinkle grated cheese on top of the egg

Leftover pasta sauces or those made with pulses or vegetables. Season them with salt and pepper or a sprinkling of soy sauce.

### FRIED EGG

Heat a tablespoon of oil in a frying pan. When it is hot break in the egg and cook over a low flame until the yolk is set. If you like the yolk cloudy, spoon over a little of the hot oil while the egg is cooking.

## SCRAMBLED EGGS AND OMELETTES

There's a certain amount of confusion between these two methods. Scrambled eggs are cooked over a low heat until they thicken and form a creamy mass, whereas omelettes are cooked quickly over a high flame and the base becomes golden brown. Some people are adept at making one kind and swear they can't do the other. To make sure of success the pan should be very clean for both methods and there should be no problems with sticking if you heat the pan and oil or butter before adding the beaten eggs. You can use margarine but you may find the eggs are more likely to stick to the base of the pan.

### HOW TO SCRAMBLE EGGS

Heat a tablespoon of oil or butter in a small saucepan over a low heat. Break 1–2 eggs into a bowl, beat with a fork until the yolks are incorporated. Add 1 teaspoon of milk or yoghurt per egg, a pinch of salt and pepper. Beat a little. When the oil or fat begins to foam and is hot, pour in the eggs and cook over a low heat. Stir gently and they will gradually thicken. As soon as they are set but still glistening they are ready. If you leave them longer they will become dry and leathery.

*Mumbled eggs* A variation of scrambled eggs. Heat the oil or butter in the pan and when it is foaming, break the eggs straight into the pan. Stir quickly with a wooden spoon to mix them. Keep stirring until they are set but still moist. Add salt and pepper to taste.

Eat scrambled eggs or mumbled eggs just as they are or with one of the fillings below.

HOW TO MAKE AN OMELETTE

Heat a frying pan over a medium heat. Beat the eggs until just mixed, add a pinch of salt and some pepper. When the pan is hot add a tablespoon of oil or butter. Raise the heat and when the oil or fat foams and splutters, pour in the egg mixture. Let it settle and begin to set. Lift the edges with an egg slice or spatula, tilting the pan so that the mixture runs underneath. Continue until the omelette is set but the top is still moist. You can add a filling such as those suggested below, fold the omelette in half, using the slice or spatula, and slide it from pan to plate.

Ideas for fillings and toppings for scrambled eggs or omelettes

*Cheese*   Stir 1–2 tablespoons of grated cheese or small pieces of curd or cottage cheese into the scrambled egg as it begins to set, or add the cheese to the omelette just before you fold it in half. If you like goat's cheese, you'll find it delicious with eggs.

*Banana*   Add chopped banana as the eggs are setting.

*Beans*   Add a tablespoon or two of any cooked pulses.

*Herbs*   Add ½ teaspoon of dried herbs such as thyme or oregano, or 1 teaspoon of fresh herbs such as parsley or mint, chives or sweet basil.

*Onion*   Add chopped onion which you have cooked in a little hot oil or butter in the pan before preparing your eggs.

*Nuts*   Add 1 tablespoon of chopped nuts such as almonds, walnuts, peanuts or pine-nuts.

*Seeds*   Add a sprinkling of sesame, sunflower or pumpkin seeds.

*Sweetcorn*    Add 2–3 tablespoons of sweetcorn.

Any of the following could be cooked, sliced or chopped according to their shape and size, in a little oil with some chopped onion or garlic before being added to the cooked scrambled eggs or folded into the omelette: courgette, mushroom, cooked potato (or grated raw potato), spinach, green or red pepper (seeds discarded), bread, spring onion, leek, beansprouts, or tomatoes.

## GRATINS AND QUICHES

You may well feel that these are not worth making if you are cooking only for yourself but the quantities given will feed two people, or do you for two meals. They are nice eaten hot or cold. Gratins made with eggs are like quiches without the pastry.

Heat the oven to Gas 5/375°F/190°C for either a gratin or a quiche.

BASIC GRATIN OR QUICHE FILLING

    2 eggs
    6 tablespoons milk, or yoghurt or 4 tablespoons curd
      cheese and 2 tablespoons milk
    salt, pepper
    pinch of nutmeg
    extra ingredient (see below)
    1–2 tablespoons grated cheese

Beat the eggs with the milk, yoghurt or curd cheese. Add salt, pepper and nutmeg. Prepare and stir in any extra ingredients.

*To fill a gratin*    Grease a heatproof dish with a little oil or butter. Pour the mixture into it, add grated cheese. Cook for 20–25 minutes in the pre-heated oven.

*To fill a quiche*    Make a pastry base as explained on page 108. Pour the mixture into it, and add grated cheese. Cook for 30–35 minutes in the pre-heated oven.

Suggested extra ingredients for gratin and quiche

Add 3–4 tablespoons of any of the following: grated cheese,

sweetcorn, any cooked pulses, cooked vegetables such as ratatouille (see page 13) or use the canned kind, or stir-fried vegetables (page 128).

Or, chop up and soften in hot oil in a wok or frying pan one of the following: onion, half a dozen or so mushrooms, green or red pepper, seeds discarded, (or use canned pimentos), 1–2 courgettes, spinach or broccoli cooked briefly in a little salted water (page 126).

Or, slice 2–3 tomatoes, sprinkle them with salt and leave them for 30 minutes to drain their excess moisture. Lay them on the pastry base, pour over the egg mixture and sprinkle the top with ½ teaspoon of marjoram or basil as well as grated cheese.

PASTRY BASE

For 18 cm (7 inch) flan tin.

> 1 mug self-raising wholemeal flour (or use plain whole-meal flour with 1 teaspoon baking powder)
> pinch salt
> 6 tablespoons fat – either vegetable shortening, or use a mixture of half butter and half vegetable shortening
> 3 tablespoons cold water, approximately

Sift the flour, baking powder and salt through a sieve, tipping in any excess bran that remains behind. If you have no sieve, don't worry. Add the fat, cutting it into the flour with a knife. When the pieces are quite small, begin to rub them into the flour using your fingers, until it becomes like fine bread-crumbs. Mixing with a knife, gradually add enough water to make a firm dough. (The amount of water varies depending on the flour.) The dough should feel spongy, not crumbly or sodden. Put some flour on your hands so the dough doesn't stick and form the dough into a ball. Freshly made dough shrinks, so set it aside for 30 minutes, covered, in a cool place. If you use it immediately it will shrink as it cooks and spoil the look of your dish. As pastry made with wholemeal flour has a tendency to crumble when it is rolled, you might find it easier to press it into the tin instead. When the dough has rested, flour your hands again and flatten the ball of dough, put it into your tin, pressing it outwards until it covers the base and sides. If you prefer to roll it, put some flour on to a board and the rolling pin and roll the dough firmly but lightly into a circle large enough to cover the base and sides of the tin. Fold the circle in half, lift it and settle it over one half of the tin, flip over the folded half. Ease the pastry from the outer edge to fit. Roll the pin over the top so that the tin edge cuts away the excess. If you want crisp pastry try brushing it with a little egg white thinned with water. Use some of the egg white before beating up the eggs with the filling mixture.

#  SALADS

You gain bonus points for eating salads in which you get all the goodness of the vegetables with hardly any work and no need to feel guilty about not bothering to cook! It really isn't at all hard to follow the counsel of perfection which is to make salads a daily feature of your diet. Have no fears that they are only for summer. It is true that there's a glut of choice then with masses of home-grown tomatoes, crisp radishes, tiny spring onions, cucumbers, boxes of mustard and cress and plenty of cheap lettuces and fresh herbs, but at other times of the year you can use less obvious ingredients, like raw, sliced mushrooms flavoured with lemon juice and garlic; white cabbage shredded with chopped red apples, sprinkled with walnuts; shredded carrot with chicory and orange slices; Chinese leaves mixed with raisins and peanuts, topped with sesame seeds.

The combinations are infinite and you can let loose your imagination. The secret is to limit yourself to no more than 3 or 4 different vegetables, contrasting those you choose in colour, taste or texture.

PREPARING VEGETABLES FOR SALADS

Prepare your salads when you are ready to eat them – in this way you retain all their natural excellence. Wash them under running cold water and don't leave them soaking as you'll end up by throwing away a lot of their goodness with the water. Peel only those vegetables which have really tough skins, and discard only fading outside leaves from lettuce and cabbages. Dark green leaves are actually the most nutritious. It is simple to tear leaves into manageable pieces; other vegetables may need chopping or shredding. If you are not going to eat all of a vegetable at once, save the root end as it will remain fresher longer.

# MAKING UP SALADS

It is actually easier to make up a salad in a bowl if you plan to eat it with some sort of dressing. The dressing can be made in the bowl, the salad ingredients added, and then the whole lot mixed so that everything is covered with dressing. If you only want a flavouring of garlic, you can achieve this by rubbing the cut edge of a clove of garlic around your bowl; or try rubbing it over a piece of stale bread and putting this into the bowl, topped by dressing and salad. The bread will become moist and be subtly flavoured. Salad dressings are on page 114.

### BEANSPROUTS

Mix with apple, spring onions, red or green peppers or sliced mushrooms, or use them to provide a crisp topping to any salad.

### COOKED BEETROOT

Try it sliced with a yoghurt and lemon dressing mixed with apple; or with hard-boiled egg, or sliced tomato, and perhaps garlic. (Greengrocers sell beetroot both ready-cooked and raw.)

### BRUSSELS SPROUTS

Slice young sprouts and mix with chopped celery or celeriac, a tablespoon of dried fruit, chopped nuts or seeds and a vinaigrette or yoghurt dressing.

### CABBAGE, RED OR WHITE

Slice finely with grated carrot, chopped celery or green peppers, mixed with chopped onion and mayonnaise or a yoghurt dressing. Top with peanuts and raisins or a chopped apple.

### CARROT

Shred or grate and mix with chopped apple and a lemon French dressing, flavoured with garlic and parsley.

### CAULIFLOWER

Break into florets, and mix with vinaigrette flavoured with a pinch of mustard or ½ teaspoon of turmeric, mixed with chopped apple.

### CELERY

Cut into 2½cm (1 inch) lengths, mix with chopped walnuts, apple and a little grated carrot, and top with slices of cheese with a vinaigrette dressing.

### CELERIAC

Grate or cut very finely and mix with vinaigrette or yoghurt dressing; use like celery.

### CHICORY

Cut into slices, add grated carrot and a peeled and sliced orange. Use a very sharp knife to peel the orange, cutting away all the bitter pith. Flavour the salad with lemon French dressing.

### COURGETTE

Slice or grate, flavour with garlic, thyme and lemon juice or yoghurt dressing, sprinkle with fresh parsley or coriander leaves chopped.

### CUCUMBER

Chop cucumber and mix it with spring onion, lemon juice and yoghurt or cottage cheese, and plenty of pepper. Top with slices of fennel.

### FENNEL

Slice and mix with grated carrot and slices of cheese, sprinkle with lemon juice and add enough oil to moisten.

### LETTUCE

As well as the familiar round and Cos lettuce, try Webb's Wonder, Chinese leaves, Iceberg and endive, which has a frizzy leaf. They are more expensive but keep well and will do for several salads.

MUSHROOMS

Slice them raw and mix with a little oil, lemon juice, salt, pepper and chopped garlic; or a dressing of yoghurt and lemon juice flavoured with mustard.

POTATO SALAD

Use potatoes boiled in their skins, slice them while still warm and add salt, pepper and a vinaigrette dressing. Or when they are cold, add some chopped garlic or onion and mix them with mayonnaise or yoghurt.

RADISHES

One of the nicest ways to eat radishes is just as they are with butter and salt.

SPINACH

Wash well and tear the leaves of young spinach into shreds. Add chopped onion or garlic, a sliced hard-boiled egg and a vinaigrette dressing.


## PASTA AND GRAINS WITH SALAD

You can use cooked pasta or grains as a base for a more substantial salad meal. Mix them with a dressing flavoured with lemon juice or vinegar and add something crisp like apple or beansprouts, celery, green or red peppers or cucumber, and contrast their pale colour with something bright like tomato and radish.

*Bulgar wheat* is used to make a famous salad which is found in Mediterranean countries under varying names and is great to make when you want a filling salad and need a quick-cooking grain as a base.

TABOULI OR TABBOULEH (2–3 servings)

Prepare half a mug of bulgar wheat as on page 69. When the grain has absorbed the water and while it is still warm, add 1 tablespoon of oil and ½ tablespoon of lemon juice or vinegar, a chopped clove of garlic and some salt and pepper. Let it cool. Add a little finely chopped onion, a sliced tomato and about a quarter of a cucumber, chopped. Add plenty of chopped fresh parsley or mint, if you have any, or if not use dried, but sparingly.

This is nice with hard-boiled eggs, or thinly sliced cheese; or use slices of tofu but soak them first in 1 tablespoon of soy sauce for about 30 minutes. Or you could eat it with curd cheese, either bought or made by yourself from yoghurt, see page 140.

## PULSES IN SALADS

Use any cooked pulses you may have available in salads. There are dozens of recipes to be found from all over the world, but basically the methods remain much the same. Mix the beans with a dressing flavoured with lemon juice or vinegar and add chopped garlic, onion, or raw leek, and mix in other items such as chopped green or red peppers, sliced tomato, hard-boiled egg, black olives, chopped apple, chopped celery, grated carrot, shredded cabbage, chopped nuts or dried fruit, sliced cooked beetroot, raw mushrooms, chopped cucumber, beansprouts, sliced orange, or chopped herbs.

## DRESSINGS

Most salads benefit by being eaten with dressings which usually contain something sharp like vinegar, lemon juice or mustard, and are often flavoured with garlic or onion.

### VINAIGRETTE OR FRENCH DRESSING

> 1 tablespoon of vinegar or lemon juice
> 3–6 tablespoons of oil
> salt, pepper

Put all the ingredients into a screw-top jar and shake well to mix. This really is the easiest way to mix this dressing, but if you have no jar, put the vinegar in a bowl, add salt and pepper and gradually beat in the oil using a fork. The amount of oil you use depends on your own taste – the more you use the gentler the result will be.

This simple basic dressing can be varied by adding all sorts of other things such as:

*Mustard*   1 teaspoon of made or ½ teaspoon of powdered
*Tomato purée*   ½ teaspoon
*Soy sauce*   1 tablespoon
*Peanut butter*   1 tablespoon
*Tahini*   1 tablespoon
*Herbs*   ½ teaspoon of chopped herbs such as parsley or mint

### YOGHURT DRESSINGS

Yoghurt makes a lovely base for dressings. Add 1–2 table-spoons to the basic vinaigrette or French dressing; or mix it with equal quantities of mayonnnaise; or mix 2 tablespoons of yoghurt with a teaspoon of vinegar or lemon juice. Add chopped herbs or garlic or chopped onion.

### COTTAGE AND CURD CHEESE DRESSINGS

Use in the same way as for yoghurt.

### SOY SAUCE

Combines well with peanut butter or tahini to make an unusual dressing. Mix 1–2 tablespoons of the sauce with the same amount of peanut butter or tahini; add a little chopped onion or garlic, 1 tablespoon of oil and a squeeze of lemon juice. Or simply mix equal quantities of soy sauce and lemon juice.

### MAYONNAISE

1 egg yolk (see page 116)
1 teaspoon made mustard
½ mug oil such as sunflower or groundnut
1–2 tablespoons lemon juice or vinegar
pinch salt, pepper

Home-made mayonnaise is, of course, superior to any that you can buy and it isn't difficult to make although there are times when the mixture becomes temperamental: the oil and egg yolk separate and you are left with a thin, curdled mess. So, first, a few tricks to help prevent this happening.

Make sure bowl, egg, oil and whisk are all at room tem-perature – take the egg from the fridge at least half an hour beforehand. If the day is humid, watch out as this sort of atmosphere seems to affect mayonnaise: try and stand in a draught. Use a bowl with a rounded bottom like a pudding basin, as this shape lends itself to the beating action. Stand the bowl on a newspaper or cloth to prevent it slipping as you beat.

Separate an egg and put the yolk in the bowl with 1 teaspoon of made mustard (the mustard will help to stabilize the oil, or you could use the same amount of made mayonnaise for the same reason). Mix well and begin to add the oil drop by drop, beating it constantly with a whisk, fork or wooden spoon, adding more only as it becomes incorporated. As the mixture thickens so you can add the oil more quickly. Keep beating despite your arm aching, and as your mayonnaise becomes thick and gleaming you can slow down and add the lemon juice or vinegar, salt and pepper. To make quite sure it does not separate as soon as your back is turned, beat in 1 tablespoon of boiling water. It will thin slightly and be less yellow, but should hold.

And if everything fails, all is not lost. Simply begin again with a clean bowl in which you put either a fresh egg yolk, 2 teaspoons of mustard or ready-made mayonnaise. Begin to beat and gradually add the curdled mixture and mayonnaise will result! Having given all these premonitions of disaster, it is likely that you will make many successive batches with no trouble at all. It is only once in a while that a mishap strikes.

*To separate eggs*  Crack the egg in half, retaining the yolk in one piece of the shell. Pour the egg backwards and forwards between the two halves, letting the white fall into a bowl.

### AIOLI OR ROUILLE

If you like garlicky or fiery sauces try these two from southern France. You can make them up as dips and eat them with sliced vegetables, or use them stirred into soups to thicken and add flavour to them. (See recipes on page 98.)

### TOFU DRESSING

Mash some tofu and mix it with a little lemon juice and oil to form a thick dressing, add a chopped clove of garlic if you like. Vary the flavour with a teaspoon of soy sauce, a little mustard, or herbs, etc.

# AVOCADO

Although you may consider this a luxury, avocados are some-times quite cheap and when they become very ripe green-grocers often reduce the price. An avocado feels soft when ready to eat. If it is at all hard, keep it for a few days to ripen. These fruits are an acquired taste, they are not at all like ordinary pears: they are not sweet and the flesh is smooth. Their taste is bland and benefits from plenty of seasoning.

## AVOCADO SPREAD

Cut an avocado in half, discard the stone, and scoop out the flesh with a spoon. Mash it with 1 tablespoon of lemon juice (the lemon juice will prevent it from blackening). Add salt, pepper, ½ teaspoon of crushed coriander and just enough oil to make a paste. Eat it in sandwiches or with pitta bread and a salad.

## STUFFED AVOCADO

Avocados are filling, so one cut in half and stuffed with something tasty will go a long way to making a meal. (Keep the cut half, with its stone, wrapped in clingfilm in the fridge. If you can rub the exposed flesh with a little lemon juice it will help to keep its colour.)

Mix up one of the salad dressings given on pages 114, stir in one of the following and pile the mixture into the centre cavity: grated carrot and raisins, chopped banana, sliced mushrooms, chopped tomato and apple, beansprouts, diced cucumber with a little onion, diced celery with chopped walnuts.

#  POTATO BASE

Who can imagine life without potatoes? The good news is we don't need to, the humble potato has now become everyone's darling as it deserves to be – praised for its provision of vitamin C, fibre, carbohydrate and even a certain amount of protein. So if potatoes are what you fancy, stick to them. You can always lose unwanted inches by cutting out the demon sugar.

You can make potatoes the base of your meal by eating them with other protein providers such as eggs, cheese or yoghurt, or a pulse, or grains, nuts or seeds. Or perhaps just a good hunk of bread spread with peanut butter, plus a fresh salad or maybe a piece of fruit to follow – a meal that is simplicity itself!

TO PREPARE POTATOES FOR COOKING

Do you find peeling potatoes a tedious chore? You need never peel another one! Most of the goodness lies next to the skins and it is madness to throw it all away. Potatoes need not just be baked or boiled in their skins, they can also be roasted, mashed, cooked in any of their different ways, all in their skins. If at first this idea seems alarming, give it a try anyway, and you will soon find you will look with surprise on those who continue to peel them. All you need to do is wash them well under running cold water, scrub them if they are very dirty, cut out any eyes or blemishes and, hey presto! they are ready for cooking. If you come across any that are turning green, throw them out as they will have become toxic.

BAKED POTATO

The simplest and perhaps the nicest way to make a potato the base for a meal is to bake it in its skin, cut it in half and fill it with something. A medium-sized potato weighing about 275 g

(10 oz) will take about an hour to cook at Gas 6/400°F/200°C. Wash the potato and cut one or two slits in the skin to prevent it bursting in the oven. If you like a crisp potato, rub a little oil over it. Put the potato on a baking sheet near the top of the oven. Use a potato baker (see page 30) if you have one.

BOILED POTATO

If you find it extravagant to bake one potato, you could boil it. Boil some water in a pan and add the cleaned potato. Put on a lid, lower the heat and let it simmer until soft – 20–30 minutes.

Potato water is especially full of goodness, so save it for stock. It will keep 2–3 days in the fridge.

Suggested fillings for jacket potatoes

You can eat baked or boiled potatoes split down the middle with some butter or margarine, yoghurt or cheese, or try one of the following ideas.

Cut the cooked potato in half, scoop out most of the flesh with a spoon and put it in a bowl. Mash it and mix it with your chosen filling. Return it to the oven for 5–10 minutes, or put under a hot grill for 4–5 minutes. If this seems like too much trouble, just pile the filling between the two halves.

*Cottage cheese*    Mix with a beaten egg, a pinch of nutmeg, salt and pepper.

*Grated cheese*    Mix 2–3 tablespoons of grated cheese with ½ teaspoon of made mustard and a beaten egg, or a tablespoon of yoghurt.

*Curd cheese*    Mix with ¼ teaspoon of herbs such as parsley, mint, or dill; add a teaspoon of sesame seeds, a clove of garlic chopped very finely, and moisten with a little milk or yoghurt.

*Hummus or any pulse spread* (see page 44)    Moisten with a little yoghurt or tomato purée.

*Lentils or other pulses*    1–2 tablespoons of any cooked or canned beans, mixed with a squeeze of lemon juice, perhaps a tablespoon of tomato purée, salt and pepper.

*Sweetcorn*    1 tablespoon of canned sweetcorn mixed with 1 tablespoon of grated cheese, cottage or curd cheese, flavoured with 1 teaspoon of chopped fresh parsley, or ½ teaspoon of dried herbs such as parsley or mint, a pinch of paprika or cayenne pepper and 1 teaspoon of soy sauce.

If you have any sauce left over from a pasta or pancake meal or vegetable dish, you could use this to fill a potato.

*Toppings for fillings*    Any of these fillings can be sprinkled with a few sesame, dill, caraway or poppy seeds, or with a little wheatgerm, grated cheese, or chopped nuts.

### EGG COOKED IN POTATO

Boil or bake a potato (Gas 6/400°F/200°C). Cut a slice from one side and hollow out sufficient of the flesh to make a space large enough to take an egg. Make sure the potato can stand flat – if necessary cut a thin piece off the base. Break an egg into the hollow and return it to the oven until the egg is set, about 10 minutes, or you could set it under a moderate grill.

Use the discarded potato for another dish, perhaps a potato omelette (see page 107) or add it to a soup pot. You can keep it covered for a day or two in the fridge.

You can scoop out very large 'beef' tomatoes in the same way to cook an egg. Use uncooked tomatoes and once the egg is added cook as above.

### BAKED POTATOES WITH SEEDS

This is a delicious way of cooking potatoes. Wash and cut them in half. Rub all over with oil and sprinkle each cut side with seeds such as sesame, fennel, caraway, poppy, aniseed, etc. To make the seeds stick, press two cut sides together, it's less messy than pressing them with your fingers. Lay them cut sides down on a greased baking sheet and bake in the oven Gas 6/400°F/200°C for about 45 minutes, until they are soft.

### SWEET POTATOES

Can be baked or boiled just like ordinary potatoes. They are delicious with butter, salt and pepper, grated cheese or yoghurt.

MASHED POTATO

Boil some potatoes as on page 119 but cut them into pieces all of about the same size, allow about 275g (10oz) per person. Drain and mash them, skins and all. Try it, it really does work! You could use either a pestle or a masher, or even the base of a bottle. Keep mashing to get rid of all the lumps and add either an egg, or some milk, yoghurt or curd cheese to make a thick, creamy purée. Beat well and season with salt, pepper and perhaps a pinch of nutmeg. If you like garlic, you can add a small clove, finely chopped.

Use mashed potato to prepare a potato pie.

POTATO PIE

Add 2–3 tablespoons of grated cheese to the potato mixture. Pile it into a greased heatproof dish, sprinkle with a teaspoon of sesame seeds mixed with 1 tablespoon of grated cheese and put under a hot grill to heat through and brown the top.

POTATO AND LENTIL PIE

Prepare the above pie but instead of the 3 tablespoons of grated cheese, mix in cooked lentils or split peas, or any cooked or canned pulses you have on hand. Flavour the mixture with, perhaps, 1 tablespoon of tomato purée, 1 teaspoon of soy sauce or miso and ¼ teaspoon of cumin powder. Top the pie with grated cheese or a mixture of wheatgerm and sesame seeds, and put under a hot grill for a few minutes to brown.

POTATO CAKES

You can use the above potato pie mixtures to make potato cakes if you prefer. Use just enough egg or yoghurt to make a soft but firm mixture and, if necessary, add a little flour. Dampen your hands to prevent the mixture sticking and form round flat cakes about 2.5cm (1 inch) thick. Sprinkle some wholemeal flour on a board; dip the cakes into it coating them all over. If possible set them aside for 15–20 minutes before you cook them as this helps them to firm up and hold their shape. Heat a frying pan and add 1–2 tablespoons of oil. As soon as it sizzles, add the cakes and fry them on both sides until golden, lowering the heat to prevent them burning.

You can make them more interesting by adding a few chopped peanuts, almonds or walnuts.

Below are some ideas that are useful if you have several mouths to feed.

### EGGS BAKED IN MASHED POTATO (4 servings)

Prepare some mashed potato, (see page 119) allowing about 150g (6oz) per person. Rub a little oil or butter over a heatproof dish, put in the mashed potato, spread it evenly and make hollows in it, each large enough to hold an egg. Break the eggs into the hollows and cook in the oven at Gas 5/375°F/190°C until the eggs are set, 8–10 minutes, or under a moderate grill for about 5 minutes.

### POTATO GRATIN (4 servings)

Grease an ovenproof dish with oil or butter. Wash and slice 4 medium potatoes thinly. (A box grater would come in handy here, as it has a slicing side.) Lay them in the dish, adding salt, pepper, 1 tablespoon of grated cheese and 1 tablespoon of sesame seeds to each layer. Beat an egg in a mug and top up with milk. Pour over the potatoes, adding a little more milk if required as the mixture should come about threequarters of the way up the side of the dish. Sprinkle 3–4 tablespoons of grated cheese over the top. Bake at Gas 6/400°F/200°C for 45 minutes until it is brown and the potatoes are soft.

### POTATO GRATIN WITH CARROT AND TOMATO (4 servings)

Wash and slice 4 medium potatoes thinly and 2–3 carrots. Open a medium can of Italian tomatoes or use 3–4 fresh tomatoes. Grease an ovenproof dish with oil or butter. Put in a layer of potatoes and carrots, pour over the tomatoes crushing them with a fork (or lay over the sliced tomatoes and add sufficient water or stock to barely cover the vegetables). Sprinkle over 1 tablespoon of soy sauce, ½ teaspoon of sweet basil, oregano or parsley and add some salt and pepper. Top with a layer of grated cheese or wheatgerm and sesame seeds, allow 2–3 tablespoons. Bake at Gas 6/400°F/200°C for 45 minutes until it is brown and the potatoes and carrots are soft.

POTATO PANCAKES (makes 2  15 cm [6 inch] pancakes)

These pancakes make a quick supper dish.

    1 potato about 225 g (8 oz)
    1 small onion, chopped
    2 tablespoons wholemeal flour
    2 tablespoons grated cheese, or curd cheese
    salt, pepper
    pinch each of powdered coriander and cumin
    1 egg
    1 tablespoon soy sauce
    1 teaspoon turmeric (optional)

Chop the onion very small. (You can grate it if you like but it may make you cry!) Mix the onion with the flour, cheese, salt, pepper, coriander and cumin. Stir in the turmeric if you are using it; it will give flavour as well as tingeing the cakes a golden yellow – without it they look a bit grey. Wash the potato and grate it, skin and all. A box grater comes in handy here. You need to get rid of as much of the liquid in the potato as you can, so squeeze it between two layers of kitchen towel. Potato discolours quickly once exposed to the air, so it is a good idea to cook these pancakes as soon as they are mixed. Add the potato to the other ingredients. Beat the egg and mix it in, beating well.

Heat a frying pan with 2 tablespoons of oil; when it is hot, drop in half the mixture. Press it out to cover the base and cook until it is golden on both sides, it will take 2–3 minutes each side. Cook the second pancake.

This is nice with yoghurt and relish if you have some or with the following sauce.

*Peanut butter and onion sauce*  Put a tablespoon of oil in a small pan and heat it. When it is hot add a chopped onion and cook over a medium heat until it just begins to brown. Add 2 tablespoons of peanut butter, 1 teaspoon of soy sauce, a squeeze of lemon juice and some pepper. Mix and serve.

## Variations

*Potato and sweetcorn pancakes*   Make some potato pancakes but add canned sweetcorn instead of the cheese. If you don't like the spices add instead some chopped herbs.

*Extra protein*   If you want, you can stir in 1 tablespoon of skimmed milk powder or 1 tablespoon soya flour to any of these potato dishes.

# ❦ VEGETABLES ❦

Many people attracted to vegetarianism begin by declaring that they could live on vegetables. It isn't quite so simple. Vegetables play a key role but as they are low in proteins, they must be eaten with protein foods: grains, nuts and seeds; pulses; dairy foods and eggs.

There is no doubt that making salads is by far the simplest and most beneficial way of eating vegetables. Cooking destroys some of their goodness but this section gives some delicious ideas for using vegetables cooked as the pivot of a meal. You could always accompany them with a simple salad. You may want to eat a cooked vegetable with some other dish you are preparing, so here is how to go about it.

## TO WASH VEGETABLES

Wash them under running cold water when you are ready to use them. Soaking reduces their nutritional value. Root vegetables may need to be scrubbed – a nylon scouring pad comes in handy – but only those with really coarse skins need to be peeled.

Green vegetables should have the outer, yellowing leaves discarded.

Prepare individual vegetables as in the chart (see page 126).

## TO COOK VEGETABLES IN WATER

Put a very little water into a pan, about 2.5cm (1 inch) deep. Bring it to the boil, add a pinch of salt. Add the prepared vegetable, cover the pan, lower the heat and cook until the vegetable is just tender, following times in the chart which follows. Drain and save the water to be used as stock for soups, etc.

FLAVOURING COOKED VEGETABLES

Try adding a tablespoon of butter or margarine and perhaps one of the following: ½ teaspoon of herbs such as parsley, thyme, or oregano; ½ teaspoon of crushed coriander or cumin; a clove of chopped garlic; a sprinkling of sesame seeds or chopped nuts; 1 tablespoon of soy sauce; a tablespoon of grated cheese, or a tablespoon of yoghurt. Many vegetables are lovely flavoured with just a squeeze of lemon juice or a pinch of nutmeg.

The following chart shows preparation and cooking times for vegetables to be cooked in water on top of the stove. Allow 100–175 g (4–6 oz) per serving.

| Vegetable | Preparation | Cooking time in minutes |
| --- | --- | --- |
| Beans, French and runner and okra | Top and tail, remove stringy bits | 10–15 |
| Broad beans and peas | Shell | 15–20 |
| Broccoli and cauliflower | Divide into florets; discard any hard stalk | 10–15 |
| Brussels sprouts | Discard outer yellowing leaves | 5–10 |
| Cabbage, white and green | Quarter or cut in strips | 5 |
| Carrots and turnips | Leave whole if new; quarter or slice if old | 10–15 |
| Celery | Cut off root, remove stringy bits from stalks. Cook whole or in slices | 10–15 |
| Courgettes | Cut off ends. Cook young ones whole or slice | 5–10 |
| Fennel | Remove tough outer layer and root. Quarter | 10–15 |

| Vegetable | Preparation | Cooking time in minutes |
|---|---|---|
| Greens | Cut in strips or cook whole | 5 |
| Jerusalem artichokes | Cook in skins | 10–15 |
| Leeks | Discard root and all but 5 cm (2 inches) of green top. Wash well by slitting in half lengthways and dunking in cold water, discard tough layers | 10–15 |
| Parsnips and swedes | Cut off ends. Skin and quarter or slice | 10–15 |
| Potatoes | Cook in skins covered with water | 20–25 |
| Spinach | Allow 175 g (8 oz) each – it shrinks a lot. Wash very well and shake off excess water. Add no extra water to cook. Cover pan tightly, and drain thoroughly | 5 |

ROASTING VEGETABLES

Just because you don't eat roast meat, there's no reason why you shouldn't sometimes have roast vegetables, especially if you are already using the oven to cook, say, a quiche or a nut loaf. The oven should be at Gas 6/400°F/200°C, but it won't matter if it is a little cooler or hotter though you may have to adjust the cooking time accordingly.

Put a layer of oil about 1¼ cm (½ inch) deep in a roasting tin and set it in the oven to heat while you prepare the vegetable. Cut pieces of a uniform size. When the oil is hot, after 5 minutes, add the vegetables, turn them over to coat them evenly in hot oil. They will take around 45–60 minutes, depending on size. You can roast potatoes or any root vegetable in this way.

*Roasted onion*   Onions can be roasted in their skins in much the same way as jacket potatoes. Spanish onions are particularly nice. Simply cut a thin slice off their tops to act as a flat base on which to stand them. Put them on a baking sheet for about 1 hour at Gas 6/400°F/200°C.

BRAISED VEGETABLES

Alternatively, vegetables may be braised in the oven. Blanch your chosen vegetable first by putting it into a pan of salted, boiling water for 4–5 minutes. Put the sliced vegetables in an ovenproof dish with enough water or stock to barely cover them. Add salt and pepper and perhaps one of the following: 1 tablespoon of soy sauce or ½ teaspoon of miso or yeast extract. Add ½ teaspoon herbs – thyme, parsley or oregano – and, if you like, a pinch of cumin, fennel or coriander. Put the dish into the oven for about 1 hour at Gas 6/400°F/200°C. Vegetables which are suitable are leeks, celery, fennel and most root vegetables, including potatoes.

## STIR-FRIED VEGETABLES

The wok is a perfect vessel in which to cook vegetables by the method of stir-frying. This is an oriental way of cooking but there is no reason why we shouldn't adapt it to our Western ideas. You can stir-fry just one vegetable as an accompaniment to something else, or you can use a mixture and make the whole operation into a meal in a pot by adding cooked grains or pulses, eggs or cheese. The wok is first heated over a medium flame. Add 1–2 tablespoons of oil which will heat very quickly so that you can begin to stir-fry – which simply means keep everything moving by stirring with a spatula or spoon.

STIR-FRYING INDIVIDUAL VEGETABLES

Wash and prepare vegetables as indicated on the chart on page 126 but cut them into smallish pieces.

As soon as the oil in the wok or pan is hot, add the vegetable and stir-fry over a medium heat for about 3 minutes. If it is a tender vegetable you can simply season it with one of the ideas on page 126 and eat it straight away. If it needs further cooking add ½ mug of water or stock, cook over a medium heat with the lid on for 5–10 minutes, and finally add seasoning.

STIR-FRYING AN ASSORTMENT OF VEGETABLES

You can be as inventive as you like with your assortment. It is usually a good idea to include an onion or leek or perhaps some garlic, and the Chinese usually add a little root ginger cut very small which gives a sweet, peppery flavour to the dish.

Begin by stir-frying the chopped onion, leek or garlic and the ginger if using. After 3 minutes add any of the harder vegetables such as roots and peppers. Stir-fry for a further 3 minutes before adding the softer ones like tomatoes or mushrooms. Continue stir-frying until all the vegetables are hot but still crisp. Sometimes it is a good idea to add just a little water or stock to the pan and put on the lid. Turn the heat down and cook for a few minutes. Add salt, pepper, 1 tablespoon of soy sauce and any other seasoning.

Additions to stir-fried vegetables

Make a meal by adding one of the following to the contents of the wok:

*Cooked grains*   Mix in half a mugful, stir well, add an egg and stir again to coat everything.

*Cooked pulses*   Mix in half a mugful, stir till hot through and top with grated cheese or small pieces of curd cheese.

*Nuts and seeds*   Add about 1 tablespoon of any chopped nuts such as cashews, peanuts, almonds, walnuts or pine-nuts. Or sprinkle over 1 teaspoon of sesame, sunflower or pumpkin seeds.

*Peanut butter or tahini*   At the end of the cooking time, stir in 1–2 tablespoons of either.

*Tofu or beancurd*   Goes well with stir-fried vegetables. Soak it for 30 minutes in 1–2 tablespoons of soy sauce. As it breaks easily, it is a good idea to fry it, cut in cubes, for 2–3 minutes after you have softened the onion etc. Remove the tofu from the pan and return it when the other ingredients are cooked.

*Beansprouts*    Add a handful of beansprouts at the end of the cooking time and stir until they are hot through.


## SOME VEGETABLE MEALS

### TOMATO AND ONION WITH EGG (and other variations)

Heat a wok or frying pan and add 2 tablespoons of oil. Cook a chopped onion, stir-frying for 2–3 minutes. Add 2 sliced tomatoes and cook 2–3 minutes longer. Make a hollow in the centre and break in an egg, cook until it is set.

Instead of tomatoes, you could use a sliced courgette, or red or green pepper. Or use beansprouts – flavour them with 1 teaspoon of soy sauce before adding the egg.

If you have some ratatouille left over (see page 131) heat it through in a wok or frying pan, stir-frying for 3 minutes, and then add the egg.

### SPINACH WITH POACHED OR STEAMED EGGS

This is a good dish to make to feed more than one, being both delicious and cheap. Cook some spinach as on page 127, poach or steam an egg for each person. Lay the well-drained spinach in a shallow heatproof dish, top with the eggs, sprinkle with grated cheese and, if you like, a few sesame seeds and put the dish under a hot grill for the cheese to melt and turn golden, 2–3 minutes.

### VEGETABLE CHEESE

Lots of people know cauliflower cheese but not that you can use other vegetables in much the same way. Just cook the vegetables as on page 126, drain them well, pour over a cheese sauce (see page 61) and place under a hot grill for a few minutes for the top to turn golden. Try using leeks, broccoli or courgettes.

VEGETABLE GRATINS

Vegetables can be used to make gratins – dishes usually topped with grated cheese or breadcrumbs, or perhaps wheatgerm and sesame seeds, or flaked oats or other grains. They are put in the oven or under a grill so that the top turns crisp and golden. There are suggestions for vegetable gratins using eggs and cheese on pages 107–8. You can also use this method to add interest to stir-fried vegetables, see page 126. Add one of the suggested toppings to the cooked vegetables in the wok or pan, dribble a little oil over the top and stick the lot under the grill for 2–3 minutes.

CORN ON THE COB

Fresh corn is in season for a few weeks in early autumn and is lovely eaten very hot with plenty of freshly milled pepper, a generous amount of butter and perhaps a little finely chopped garlic. Remove the outer leaves and silky fibres. Half fill a pan with water (do not add salt as it will prevent the seeds from softening). Bring it to the boil, add the corn and let it simmer, covered, until soft (about 20 minutes). Put the whole cob on your plate and if you like push a fork into each end, to make it easier to hold. Add your seasonings and eat the seeds straight from the cob – the husk is definitely not for eating.

*Corn on the cob baked*   Wrap each prepared cob loosely in a piece of foil and bake in a hot oven Gas 6/400°F/200°C for 15–20 minutes. A handy method if the oven is already being used.

## VEGETABLE STEWS

The following two ideas are really for several people. The first is for making in summer when all the vegetables which owe their origins to the Mediterranean countries are in season.

RATATOUILLE

This dish comes from southern France where every cook has their own version. It is simply a conglomeration of onions, aubergines, courgettes, sweet peppers and tomatoes cooked together in a pot, flavoured with plenty of herbs and garlic. It is wonderful eaten hot or cold. If there is any over, which is rare, you could use it as quiche or gratin filling, on its own or mixed with grains or pulses, or try the recipe with eggs (see below).

The quantities given in the recipe will make enough for 4 servings. There is absolutely no hard and fast rule as to exactly how many or how much of each of the vegetables you need. Make it first my way and then do it again using your own quantities.

    3 tablespoons oil
    1 onion, chopped
    2 cloves of garlic, chopped
    2 aubergines
    2 courgettes
    1 green or red pepper
    4 tomatoes or 1 can of Italian tomatoes, drained
    1 teaspoon thyme, marjoram and parsley
    salt, pepper

Heat a large saucepan and add the oil. When it is hot add the chopped onion and let it soften for a few minutes, stirring. Add the garlic, aubergines and courgettes cut into slices about ½cm (¼ inch) thick. Mix them well and let them cook for about 5 minutes. Add the pepper, sliced, seeds discarded, the tomatoes, herbs, salt and pepper. Stir well. Bring to the boil, cover, lower the heat and cook for about 40 minutes. There is no need to add any extra liquid because the aubergine, courgettes and tomatoes have plenty of moisture of their own.

Eat ratatouille with a cooked grain and plenty of grated cheese, or add half a mugful of cooked pulses to the pot.

Or eat it with one of the cooked pulse and rice dishes given on pages 87 and 88.

*Ratatouille with eggs*   When the ratatouille is cooked, break in 1–2 eggs per person and let them cook very gently over a low heat until they are set. Delicious!

COUS-COUS

This recipe also comes from the South of France although the dish originates from North Africa. It combines grain in the

form of cous-cous with a pulse – chickpeas – and an assortment
of vegetables. The grain is steamed over the stew of chickpeas
and vegetables, thus absorbing their taste and flavour.
Obviously you won't have a *couscousier* – the special pot and
steamer used for this dish – but you can use a metal colander
instead providing it sits comfortably over a saucepan. If this is
impossible, cook the grain separately as described under
Method 1 on page 69. The finished dish is eaten with a fiery
sauce made with *harissa* which is a paste flavoured strongly
with chillies sold in tubes. You may find it in delicatessens or
Asian shops; if not, use a bottled hot chilli sauce. The following
recipe comes from a friend, Monique, who lives in the Languedoc. She includes meat, so I have adapted it a little and
added cumin and coriander to make it more tasty.

Don't be alarmed by the long list of ingredients, the dish is
easy to make and inexpensive. It serves 4 people.

    2 tablespoons oil
    2–3 onions
    2 leeks
    2 turnips
    4 carrots
    1 green or red pepper
    4 medium potatoes
    2 courgettes
    water to cover
    2 mugs cous-cous
    4 mugs boiling water
    ½ teaspoon salt
    1 clove of garlic
    2 chillies or ½ teaspoon cayenne pepper
    1 teaspoon paprika
    ½ teaspoon cumin
    ½ teaspoon coriander
    salt, pepper
    1 can Italian tomatoes
    2 mugs cooked chickpeas, or 2 cans
    2–3 tablespoons butter or oil
    3–4 tablespoons raisins, optional
    1–2 tablespoons *harissa* or other hot chilli sauce

Heat the oil in a large saucepan (over which you can fit a metal colander if you have one). Prepare and slice the onions, leeks, turnips, carrots, green or red pepper, potatoes and cour- gettes. Add all these to the pan; stir and cook for several minutes. While they are cooking, put the 2 mugs of cous-cous into a bowl and pour over 4 mugs hot or boiling water, add ½ teaspoon of salt, put a plate on top and leave for the grain to swell.

To the vegetables in the pot, add the chopped garlic, chop- ped chillies or cayenne pepper, paprika, cumin and coriander, crushed or powdered, salt and pepper and enough water to not-quite cover the vegetables. Bring it to the boil. Empty the cous-cous into a colander – if the holes seem too big, line it with a piece of muslin or a clean tea-towel. Set the colander over the pan, cover and simmer for 20 minutes.

Take the colander off, add the tomatoes and chickpeas to the vegetables. Cut the butter into small pieces and add to the cous-cous with the raisins if using, stir with a fork. Put it back on the pan and cook for a further 20 minutes.

Make the hot sauce by mixing the *harissa* or hot chilli sauce with some of the liquid from the stew. Serve this separately: it is very hot and some people may prefer to do without.

If you wish, serve any other sort of grain with this vegetable and chickpea stew.

The Spanish make a dish called cocido which is quite similar to cous-cous. It is not so fiery and the vegetables are added to the pot in which the pulse is cooking. The recipe is on page 91.

## STUFFED VEGETABLES

Many vegetables provide perfect receptacles for stuffings and you can cook a whole meal in such containers. The stuffing mixture can be made from cooked pulses, grains, or nuts flavoured with onion and other vegetables, and some are nice with a simple egg and cheese filling.

Below are three simple stuffings which you could adapt to suit the ingredients you have in stock.

PULSE AND GRAIN STUFFING (2 servings)

> 1 tablespoon oil
> 1 onion
> 1 clove of garlic
> 3 tablespoons cooked grain
> 3 tablespoons cooked pulse
> salt, pepper
> ¼ teaspoon herbs such as thyme, oregano or parsley
> 1 teaspoon tomato purée

Heat the oil in a wok or frying pan and add the chopped onion. Let it soften for 3–4 minutes. Add all the other ingredients and mix well.

NUT STUFFING (2 servings)

Make as for the above stuffing but use 4 tablespoons of cooked grain and 2 tablespoons of chopped nuts such as peanuts, almonds, walnuts, cashews or pine-nuts.

Variations on stuffings

Instead of cooked grains you can use breadcrumbs or wheat-germ or rolled oats. You could add 1 tablespoon of dried fruit such as raisins; or try adding spices like ¼ teaspoon of cumin or coriander. For hotness, add a pinch of cayenne, or for a mild spiciness ½ teaspoon of paprika. Instead of tomato purée (or as well) add 1 teaspoon of soy sauce or ½ teaspoon of miso or yeast extract.

EGG AND CHEESE FILLING (2 servings)

This filling is most suitable to fill vegetables with deep cavities, which makes it ideal for peppers or tomatoes.

> 4 tablespoons curd cheese
> 1 teaspoon flour
> 1 egg
> 2 tablespoons grated cheese
> salt, pepper
> a little milk or yoghurt

Mix the curd cheese with the flour, beaten egg, 1 tablespoon of grated cheese, salt, pepper and enough milk or yoghurt to make a mixture like thick, whipped cream. Fill your chosen vegetable and sprinkle the remaining grated cheese on top. Use oven cooking method.

## PREPARING AND FILLING THE VEGETABLES

The chart that follows gives the various ways of dealing with vegetables which are suitable for stuffing. Pile your prepared filling into the hollows in the vegetables and cook in one of the following ways:

*In the oven*   Heat oven to gas 5/375°F/190°C. Take a shallow heatproof dish and pour in 2–3 tablespoons of stock or water, flavoured with 1 tablespoon of soy sauce or tomato purée. Lay the filled vegetables in the dish and top them with either grated cheese, breadcrumbs, wheatgerm or a mixture, and perhaps a sprinkling of sesame seeds or chopped nuts. Dribble a little oil over and put in the oven for specified time.

*On top of the stove*   Use a saucepan and add enough water to come half-way up the vegetable, flavoured with 1 tablespoon of soy sauce or tomato purée – or you could simply empty in the contents of a can of Italian tomatoes, crushing the tomatoes a little.

Put in the vegetable and cook, covered, on a low heat for specified time.

*Grilled*   This method is suitable for mushrooms or tomatoes. In the case of mushrooms, melt 1 tablespoon of butter in the grill pan, put in the mushrooms and turn them to coat with the fat. Leave under the hot grill for 2–3 minutes to soften, pile in the hot stuffing, top with grated cheese or breadcrumbs, or wheatgerm and sesame seeds, and replace under the grill for 3–4 minutes more.

If using tomatoes, fill them with the hot stuffing; add a topping as for mushrooms, sprinkle with a little oil and put under a moderate grill to cook the tomatoes and brown the topping.

Preparation, method of cooking and times for various stuffed vegetables

| Vegetable | Preparation | Cooking method(s) | Times in minutes |
|---|---|---|---|
| Aubergine ½ medium one each | Cut in half lengthwise, scoop out the pulp with a spoon. Chop the flesh and mix with the stuffing | { Oven<br>{ Top of stove | 30–40 |
| Cabbage, Chinese leaves, Spinach, etc. Allow 3–4 outer leaves each | Blanch the leaves 3 minutes.* Put stuffing in centre of each leaf, roll up or fold like a parcel | { Oven<br>{ Top of stove | 30 |
| Courgette 1 each | Prepare as aubergine | { Oven<br>{ Top of stove | 30–40 |
| Marrow 30 cm (12 inch) in length will feed 3–4. Double amount of stuffing | Cut in half lengthwise, scoop out the seeds with a spoon. Blanch 5 minutes.* Fill each half, tie together with thread or string | Oven | 60 |
| Mushrooms 1 very large or 2 medium each | Cut off stalks, chop and mix with stuffing. Coat mushrooms in melted butter (1 tablespoon) before filling | { Oven<br>{ Grill | 15–20<br>5–10 |
| Peppers | Either cut in half lengthwise, or cut off the top and use as a cap. Discard seeds and blanch 5 minutes* | { Oven<br>{ Top of stove | 30 |
| Tomatoes 1 very large or 2 medium each person | Cut large ones in half round middle, or cut top off medium and use as a cap. Scoop out centres with a spoon, chop and add to stuffing | { Oven<br>{ Grill | 15–20<br>5–10 |

*Blanching is putting the vegetable into a pan half full of boiling salted water. It helps to soften the vegetable and make it more malleable.

# 🍃YOGHURT AND CURDS🍃

## YOGHURT

Read almost anything about yoghurt and invariably you will be told that in Bulgaria, where it is eaten in large amounts, there are more people who have lived to be a hundred than anywhere else. Then the doubts creep in and no one is sure whether it is the yoghurt or living in Bulgaria which has this happy result.

It is, however, known that yoghurt, as well as containing a high proportion of protein, provides some calcium and contains a bacillus which effectively eliminates undesirable bacilli in the digestive system.

Yoghurt has a subtle, acidic taste which may take time to acquire. Once acquired, however, you will find yoghurt endlessly useful. It makes muesli luxurious, is lovely in soups or mixed with cooked vegetables. It makes light salad dressings and is delicious on its own, with fresh or dried fruit or sweetened with a little honey. Avoid the commercial varieties which are artificially coloured or flavoured, and buy natural yoghurt – or save some money by making your own. It takes only a few moments and you can make sufficient in one batch to last several days.

Although you may have seen yoghurt starters in some shops, you can make it by using a spoonful of any natural yoghurt (not pasteurized). After the first batch, you make each successive batch using a spoonful of your own yoghurt. If the result begins to seem less good, start again with a fresh carton.

TO MAKE YOGHURT

    1 pint long-life or sterilized milk
    2 tablespoons skimmed milk powder
    1 tablespoon ready-made plain yoghurt

The easiest way to make yoghurt is to use a wide-mouthed vacuum flask which holds ½ litre (1 pint). You can use a smaller one but it saves time to make a larger amount. If you have no flask, you can use a bowl which you should cover and leave somewhere warm and out of draughts.

Make sure that the flask or bowl is scrupulously clean and to be certain, rinse them out with boiling water.

*Method*   Heat the milk to blood heat which means that when you dip your finger in, you should be able to count to 10 before you need to pull it out. Put the yoghurt and skimmed milk powder into the flask or bowl, and mix them. Add the milk, stirring well. Put on the top or cover the bowl with a clean cloth and leave it somewhere warm for 4–8 hours. The longer it is left the thicker but more tart it will become. When it is set, it should be put in the fridge if possible (turn it out of the flask) where it will thicken more. If you have no long-life, use ordinary pasteurized milk but it must first be boiled and then allowed to cool to blood heat. You can leave out the skimmed milk powder if you prefer a thin, runny yoghurt.

*Curds and whey*   Once in a while something goes wrong and the mixture separates into curds and whey. Don't throw it away. Use the curds to make cheese (see page 140) and the whey (the liquid) can be added to soup or sauces.

## Variations

*Yoghurt with water and skimmed milk powder*   Make up ½ litre (1 pint) of milk using water and skimmed milk powder as the instructions on the container. Make as for fresh milk, which means that you must bring it to the boil and let it cool to blood heat. Mix 1 tablespoon of yoghurt with 2 tablespoons of skimmed milk powder and pour over the mixed milk, stirring well. Continue as usual.

*Yoghurt with soya milk*   If you are a vegan, you can make yoghurt in exactly the same way as for fresh milk using soya milk. If you start it with ordinary yoghurt, the first batch won't be strictly vegan, but subsequent batches will.

*Yoghurt instead of cream*   You can use yoghurt instead of cream in many recipes. Don't let it boil as it will curdle.

## CURD CHEESES, ALSO SOLD AS QUARK

Curd cheeses, which are usually made from cow's milk, are becoming more and more commonplace. They are soft textured with a delicate flavour and can be used to make sauces, in omelettes or scrambled eggs, stirred into soups, in sandwiches, as part of salads and even at breakfast time. In other parts of the world curd cheeses are to be found made from goat's, ewe's and even buffalo's milk, and each has its own special flavour.

Curd cheese is simple to make but time-consuming and not very cost effective. However, a very quick curd cheese can be made using yoghurt, and if you like the idea of trying new flavours, you can try making it from Greek yoghurt which is made from goat's or ewe's milk, or search out home-produced ones which are sometimes sold in country areas. You can, of course, use your home-made yoghurt to make cheese.

CURD CHEESE FROM YOGHURT

> a piece of muslin, cheesecloth, or J-cloth
> a 1-litre (2-pint) wide-mouthed jar
> a rubber band
> a pencil
> a colander or sieve
> 225 g (8 oz) natural yoghurt

Lay the cloth in the colander and empty the yoghurt into it. Bring up the corners to form a bag and fasten with the rubber band. Hang the bag on the pencil and suspend the bag inside the jar, the pencil across the opening. (If you haven't got a jar, you can just hang the bag over a bowl, if there is a convenient hook from which to suspend it.) Leave it overnight or for about 8 hours. The moisture or whey will drip into the jar and the curd will be left in the bag.

Add the whey to soups or sauces. Empty the cheese into a bowl and sprinkle with a pinch of salt, and keep it covered in the fridge for up to 3 days.

Some suggestions for using curd cheese

*Grilled curd cheese*  Toast bread on one side only, spread

untoasted side with curd cheese, sprinkle with a little oil and put under a hot grill.

*Curd cheese with oil* Put the cheese into a bowl, pour over 1 tablespoon of oil, add a whole red chilli, a bayleaf and a sprinkling of herbs such as thyme or marjoram. Leave covered, but not in the fridge, for a day. The cheese absorbs all the flavours and is delicious eaten with a tomato salad.

You can use this method with goat's cheese and it is a great way of livening up stale cheese.

*Stuffed vegetables* Curd cheese is used in a filling for stuffed peppers and tomatoes. The recipe is on page 135.

*Cottage cheese* This is similar to curd cheese but has a lumpy texture. You can use it in all the ways you would use curd cheese.

*Fromage frais* A very delicate curd cheese imported from France. It has a light, smooth texture and is particularly delicious with fruit of all kinds and especially the soft summer fruits like raspberries and strawberries. It can also be stirred into soups and used for cooking.

## TOFU

This is a kind of curd which is made from soya milk. It can be used just like curd cheese in most recipes but it does not melt in the same way, and because it has very little flavour requires generous seasoning. It is sold in wholefood, health shops, and some delicatessens as well as in oriental shops.

There are two forms. The first is a block with a firm, spongy texture which is easy to cut and which holds its shape during the short time it takes to cook. A smoked variety is also available. The second is sold in cartons, is less firm and is known as silken tofu. This is useful for salad dressings and for adding to soups and sauces.

The block form will keep for a month unopened. Once opened it should be stored in a fridge and kept covered in cold water to prevent a skin forming. It will then keep for a week. Silken tofu has a shelf-life similar to long-life milk; once opened it must be used within a couple of days.

You will find recipes for tofu in Japanese cookbooks and for doufu in Chinese. It is especially useful for people on a vegan diet but it also has a place in a vegetarian diet as it is high in nutrients, needs only a short time to cook and absorbs the flavour of whatever it accompanies. If you find the flavour too bland, try soaking it for half an hour in a little soy sauce.

## Suggestions for serving tofu

*Tofu in salad*    Slice a piece of tofu and add it to a salad such as grated carrots with sultanas. Pour over a vinaigrette dressing flavoured with soy sauce.

*Tofu with pasta and other sauces*    Instead of cheese, add slices of tofu.

*Tofu in sandwiches*    Mash tofu and mix it with 1–2 teaspoons of soy sauce and perhaps one of the following: peanut butter, tahini, mashed cooked pulses, tomato purée or ketchup, honey, maple syrup, a sprinkling of sesame seeds, dried fruit, and, of course, any sort of salad ingredient.

*Stir-fried tofu*    Include tofu with stir-fried vegetables. Cut small cubes of tofu and, if you like, soak them for about 30 minutes in a tablespoon of soy sauce. (See page 129 under stir-frying for how to cook.)

*Tofu dressing*    see page 116.

TOFU BURGER

> Slice of tofu about 2½ cm (1 inch) thick
> 1 teaspoon soy sauce
> 1 tablespoon cooked grain, or breadcrumbs, or wheat-germ mixed with 1 teaspoon sesame seeds
> ½ teaspoon tomato purée
> pinch herbs such as thyme or oregano
> 1 teaspoon raisins, optional

Mash the tofu, add the soy sauce and all the other ingredients. Mix well and with wet hands form the mixture into a flat burger. Set aside for half an hour to firm up and for the tofu to absorb the flavours. Fry in a little oil until golden on both sides.

# 🍃 FRUIT FOR PUDDING 🍃

Fruit is perfect for pudding. Eat it fresh and raw and you need to do very little more than wash it under the tap. This is the best way of getting all the goodness. Sometimes, though, it is nice to treat yourself and friends to something a little special and fruit can be used to make all sorts of puddings which require little time or effort. If you fancy something more elaborate and are keen on making cakes and biscuits, you will find no difficulty in searching recipes out from other cookery books.

Instead of cream

Cream is expensive and it is hard to think of eating some of the summer fruits like strawberries and raspberries without it. Yoghurt is an obvious choice – the Greek stirred variety is especially good – and look out for smetana which is a thickened culture of milk and is sold by some supermarkets as well as in Jewish delicatessens. Look out too for fromage frais which is imported from France. This is a fine, delicate curd which is lovely with fruit of any kind. You could use it to make a gooseberry or rhubarb fool, delicious treats for friends.

GOOSEBERRY OR RHUBARB FOOL (3–4 servings)

> 500 g (1 lb) green gooseberries or rhubarb
> 4 tablespoons brown sugar
> 6 tablespoons fromage frais (or use double or Devonshire cream!)

Prepare the fruit. Gooseberries: pull off tops and tails; rhubarb: cut the stalks into 5-cm (2-inch) pieces, and discard all the leaf which is poisonous.

Put the fruit into a pan with a very little water, just enough so it won't burn. Bring it to the boil, lower the heat and simmer covered until the fruit is soft, for 10–15 minutes. Stir in the sugar and let it cool. Crush into a pulp (you could use a mortar and pestle). Stir in the fromage frais or cream.

### FRIED APPLE OR BANANA

Slice the fruit. Heat the butter in a pan, add the fruit and turn it over and over. Eat it with yoghurt, a squeeze of lemon juice, perhaps a little honey and some chopped nuts or dried fruit sprinkled over.

### BAKED BANANAS

Bananas can be baked in their skins. Set the oven at Gas 5/375°F/ 190°C. Prick the skins with a fork and then put the bananas on a baking sheet near the top of the oven. Cook until they turn black, about 15–20 minutes.

Slit them down the middle and eat with honey and yoghurt or fromage frais or smetana.

### BAKED APPLES

Use Bramley cooking apples, one per person. Cut out the core and fill it with either dried fruit or chopped nuts plus a little honey; or mix curd cheese with honey and a sprinkling of sesame seeds. Bake for about 40 minutes at Gas 4/350°F/180°C. in a shallow dish with just a little water in the bottom.

### FRUIT CRUMBLES

A mixture of apple and banana makes a delicious crumble, or apples are nice with blackberries; or you can use rhubarb, plums, or apricots. You need about 450g (1 lb) fruit for 4 people. Peel and slice if necessary and lay in a shallow heat-proof dish. Sprinkle over the topping and bake Gas 5/375°F/ 190°C for 30–40 minutes.

The easiest way to make a topping is to melt 6 tablespoons of butter, margarine or oil in a pan and stir in, off the heat, 1 mug of one of the following: rolled oats, breadcrumbs, wheatgerm, muesli base, crushed biscuit crumbs, plus 6 tablespoons of sugar. Or you can rub 6 tablespoons of butter into 1 mug of flour and add 6 tablespoons of sugar.

### BREAD PUDDING

Use the same sort of fruit as for a crumble, or use a handful of dried fruit (chop the larger kinds). Lay buttered slices of bread in a shallow oven dish, top with the fruit and lay more buttered bread on top, fat side up. Beat 2 eggs with 1 mug of milk and pour over the top. Leave for 30 minutes if possible before cooking. Bake at Gas 4/350°F/180°C for 30 minutes. Take out the pudding, sprinkle the top with sugar and return to the oven for 10 minutes.

### AUTUMN PUDDING

Make this the day before you plan to eat it.

Use a mixture of blackberries and apples, about 675 g (1½ lbs) fruit in all. Slice the apples and put them into a saucepan with the blackberries, half a mug of sugar and 1 tablespoon of water. Bring to the boil and simmer for about 5 minutes.

Take a small deep bowl and line the bottom and sides with thin slices of wholemeal bread. Put in half the fruit and a layer of bread; top with the remaining fruit and cover with a final layer of bread. Seal the bowl with clingfilm and place over this a saucer or small plate – one which just fits on top. Weight it down with something heavy like a can. Leave the pudding until next day in a cool place. To serve, turn it out on to a plate. This is lovely with fromage frais, smetana or cream.

*Summer pudding* This is made the same way as Autumn pudding but use summer fruits like raspberries and redcurrants instead of blackberries.

### FRUIT CROWDIE

This is made with toasted oatmeal, sugar and fruit, mixed with cream. You can use any sort of soft fruit, or grate hard fruit like apple. Toast 1–2 tablespoons of oats in a hot frying pan until they are golden. Let it cool, mix it with 1 tablespoon of sugar, fruit and some cream, yoghurt or fromage frais.

### GRAPEFRUIT

Delicious grilled. Try the pink ones, if you can find them – they are sweeter than the yellow.

Cut the grapefruit in half round the equator and cut between each section to loosen the flesh. Sprinkle them with brown sugar and a pinch of nutmeg or cinnamon, put under a hot grill for 3–4 minutes.

## PEARS

Try eating pears with blue cheese. Or you might get hold of some very hard ones cheaply, which you can cook in apple juice: they will turn pale gold.

500 g (1 lb) hard pears
½ mug brown sugar
1 mug water
1 mug apple juice

Put the sugar and water into a pan and set it over a medium heat. As soon as it boils, lower the heat and allow to simmer until the sugar dissolves. Skin the pears thinly, leaving the stalks on. Put them in the pan with the apple juice. Bring to the boil, lower the heat and let them simmer for about 30–40 minutes. Let them cool in the pan. Put them in a bowl and leave them to get cold in the fridge.

## DRIED FRUIT

In winter when fresh fruit is scarce or expensive you can buy dried fruit. If you go to a wholefood or health shop you will find a huge selection. Don't be too alarmed by the price. When the fruit is soaked, it swells to three or four times its volume, so a small package will provide you with enough for several days. Sun-dried fruit is the best as it retains almost all the goodness of the fresh fruit; it tends to look shrivelled and unappetizing compared with sulphur-dried fruits, but these have usually been sprayed with mineral oil to make them glisten attractively. This unfortunately has the effect of preventing us from assimilating the vitamins in the fruit. To overcome this problem, wash the fruit in hot water which will remove the mineral oil. (See page 38 for preparing dried fruit.) Try eating it with curd cheese, sprinkled with lemon juice.

## SUMMER FRUITS

Summer fruits are at their best when treated simply. Each has its own particular season and as these are so short, it is good to indulge yourself while you can.

### MELON

As refreshing as a cool drink on a hot summer's day. Instead of sugar, try sprinkling it with a little freshly ground pepper. Water melons are often sold in slices which is useful when you want just enough for one. Melons should be firm, but press the top by the stalk, it should feel spongy but springy. You can also test a melon by smelling it – an unripe melon has no scent.

### STRAWBERRIES

Lovely just dipped in sugar, but they are also surprisingly good with pepper – the spicy flavour contrasts beautifully with the sweetness of the fruit. One of the most delicious summer puddings is *strawberry shortbread*.It is very easy to make and will delight everyone who is able to inveigle a slice.

> 1 mug wholemeal flour
> 100g (4oz) butter
> 4 tablespoons brown sugar

Put the flour into a bowl and add the butter cut in small pieces. Rub the butter into the flour until it looks like bread-crumbs; stir in the sugar. Using a knife, and then your hands, press the mixture into a dough. Take an 18-cm (7-inch) flan tin (or ring on a baking sheet) and press the mixture over the base. Heat oven to Gas 3/325°F/160°C and bake for 20–25 minutes. Turn out when cold. When it is cold pile 225g (8oz) strawberries on top mixed with a small carton of whipped double cream, sweetened with 1 teaspoon sugar.

*To whip cream*    Pour double or whipping cream into a round-bottomed bowl like a pudding basin. Tilt the bowl and using a fork, rounded edge downwards, and with a circular motion begin to whip the cream. The idea is to lift the cream to incorporate air. Your arm will ache, but keep going, and soon the cream will begin to thicken and rise. If you have a balloon whisk, this will be quicker.

RASPBERRIES

One of the loveliest fruits with one of the shortest seasons. If you have been making mayonnaise and have some egg whites over, you could make the simply extravagant *Hazelnut meringue cake*

> 2 egg whites
> 4 oz soft brown sugar
> ¼ teaspoon vinegar
> 3 tablespoons toasted ground hazelnuts (see page 75)

First line the base of an 18-cm (7-inch) flan tin (or use a ring on a baking sheet) with a circle of greaseproof or silicone paper, and rub butter round the edges of the tin. Heat the oven to Gas 5/375°F/190°C. Use a bowl with a rounded base like a pudding basin and make sure it is absolutely grease free. Put in the egg whites and using a fork or a balloon whisk and a circular motion, begin to beat them. They will turn white, become full of air bubbles and begin to thicken and stiffen. As soon as they are thick enough to stand in peaks, add the sugar a tablespoon at a time, and finally the vinegar. Add the hazelnuts using a spoon and a folding action, so that you don't lose any of the air in the egg whites. Lay the mixture over the base of the tin and bake for 30 minutes.

Whip a small carton of double cream (or use fromage frais), mix in 100 g (4 oz) raspberries, and reserve a further 100 g (4 oz).

When the base is cold, turn it out of the tin, pile with the raspberry and cream mixture, and arrange the remaining raspberries on top.

#  DRINKS

If you are going to be a purist you will have to forswear tea, coffee, chocolate and alcohol as they all contain stimulants which cause nasty side-effects like nervous tension, insomnia, depression. They also, of course, wake you up, keep you going when you are drowsing over some particularly tedious piece of work, and are part of our culture. The drinks in this section are given for those times when you really would like something else. Some of them will surprise you and you will certainly find that you will crave less and less of the demon caffeine.

## HERB OR SEED TEAS

The flower heads, leaves and seeds of many plants make wonderfully, refreshing teas and they are just as easy to make as ordinary tea. They are usually drunk without any milk and if you like them sweet, try adding ½ teaspoon of honey.

Herb teas can be bought either in bags or loose. Bags are more convenient but loose is cheaper.

It's a good idea to have a small teapot which you use only for herb or seed teas, as the tannin in ordinary tea pervades whatever it is made in and would spoil the delicate taste. You might instead find a *tisanière* which is a special cup or mug with its own fitted strainer all made in china. These are sometimes sold in specialist tea shops and come from France, where herb teas are called *tisanes*.

### TO MAKE HERB TEA

Allow 1 teaspoon of the herb tea per cup, pour boiling water over it and leave to infuse for about 5 minutes. Don't let it stew, or the flavour will be spoilt.

There are masses of herbs from which to choose. Try camomile or linden which are made from dried flowerheads; or peppermint, comfrey, lemon verbena or nettle-leaf teas; rosehip or Chinese jasmine.

### TO MAKE SEED TEAS

These teas are made by crushing the seeds, using 1 teaspoon per cup. Use your mortar and pestle if you have one. Put the seeds in a pan with 1 mug of cold water, bring to the boil and simmer for 10 minutes to extract the flavour. Use fennel, caraway or aniseed.

All these teas are nice with a slice of lemon and perhaps ½ teaspoon or so of honey. Vary the flavour by adding a pinch of nutmeg or cinnamon either powdered or grated.

### INSTEAD OF COFFEE

If you are keen on really fresh coffee, there is no substitute but if you normally drink instant coffee you might find one of these coffee substitutes rather better. They are usually made of dandelion root or grain and are sold in health shops; follow instructions on packets.

## WINTER WARMERS

### CAROB INSTEAD OF CHOCOLATE

If you want to avoid the caffeine in chocolate, try using carob instead which is sold in blocks as well as powdered. It has a strange bittersweet flavour all its own and makes a pleasing drink as well as being useful in recipes which specify chocolate.

Mix 2 teaspoons of carob powder with a little cold milk to form a thin paste. Pour over a mug of milk which has not quite reached boiling point. Keep stirring so that lumps don't form. Pour the mixed drink back into the pan and heat till it simmers. Try adding a sprinkling of cinnamon or a small piece of the bark, and if it doesn't seem sweet enough, add a little honey.

POSSETS

This comforting name was used for drinks made with hot milk, flavoured with spices and curdled with ale, wine or treacle. They were drunk to help cure colds. Heat a mug of milk and add a shot of ale or wine and flavour it with any of the following: 1 teaspoon of treacle, 2 teaspoons of honey, 1 teaspoon of honey and 1 of wheatgerm, or 2 teaspoons of any jam.

Flavour with a little nutmeg or cinnamon.

LEMON OR ORANGE JUICE WITH HONEY

Another comforter for colds is to squeeze the juice from an orange or lemon, top up with boiling water which you pour over the back of a spoon if using a glass to prevent it cracking. Stir in 1–2 teaspoons of honey and, if you have some, a dash of whisky.

EGG NOG

Break an egg into a glass, pour over hot milk, and sweeten with 1 teaspoon of honey.


## SUMMER REFRESHERS

FRUIT JUICE

Look out for cartons of fresh, unsweetened fruit juice which do not contain colourings or preservatives. Ideally, fruit juice should be home-made but this is a counsel of perfection and calls for a blender or food processer. If you are lucky enough to have one of these, the instruction books usually have plenty of suggestions.

*Tomato juice*   Nice with a squeeze of lemon juice or a few drops of vinegar. Try mixing equal quantities of *grapefruit and tomato juice* and drink it with a slice of lemon. This is called *Slim Jim* if you add a few drops of Worcester sauce.

*Citron pressé*   Do as the French do. Squeeze the juice of a lemon into a glass, add lots of ice, top up with water and add sugar to taste. This is wonderfully refreshing on a hot summer's day. If you have mineral water, so much the better.

### ORANGE OR LEMONADE

Put 2 mugs of boiling water into a bowl. Grate the rind of 2 oranges or 2 lemons into it – don't include any of the pith or it will be bitter. Add 2–3 tablespoons of sugar. Cover and leave overnight.

Next day, cut the fruit in half and squeeze the juice into the bowl. Taste and if necessary add a little more sugar. Dilute with water to taste.

### LEMON BARLEY WATER

This is lovely to keep in the fridge during the hot summer months. You put 4 tablespoons of barley flakes into a bowl, add 1 tablespoon of sugar, the juice of 1 lemon or 1 orange and the fruit itself. Pour over 1 mug of boiling water. Leave overnight. Strain and keep cool. Dilute with water.

You can substitute oatmeal if you have no barley flakes.

## YOGHURT DRINKS

This is likely to raise cries of ugh! from those who have never thought of using yoghurt as a drink. I first had it in Persia where it was sold in bottles and called . . .

### ABELIDOH

Put two tablespoons of yoghurt into a glass and add soda water up to the top, mixing well.

### LASSI

Made in India using plain water in place of the soda water and flavoured with a pinch of salt and cumin.

### YOGHURT AND FRUIT JUICE

Mix equal quantities of yoghurt with fruit juice.

# INDEX